ANCIENT PSALMS FOR CONTEMPORARY PILGRIMS
A PRAYER BOOK

Smyth & Helwys Publishing, Inc.
6316 Peake Road
Macon, Georgia 31210-3960
1-800-747-3016

Library of Congress Cataloging-in-Publication Data

Miley, Jeanie.
Ancient Psalms for contemporary pilgrims: a prayer book / Jeanie Miley.
p. cm.
ISBN 1-57312-390-0 (alk. paper)
1. Bible. O. T. Psalms—Meditations.
I. Title.
BS1430.54 .M55 2002
242'.5—dc21

2002151535

Ancient Psalms for Contemporary Pilgrims

a prayer book

Jeanie Miley

Dedicated
with my deepest love and gratitude

to the women
of the
Thursday Morning Bible Study
of
River Oaks Baptist Church
in Houston, Texas,
whose open minds and open hearts
challenge and stretch me,
giving me courage and deep joy . . .

and to the monks
of
St. Benedict's Monastery,
Snowmass, Colorado,
whose faithful prayers and sacred spaces
have instilled in me
a deep awareness
the reality
of
the ineffable Mystery of God
in the
ordinary things of life.

I am forever blessed by these fellow pilgrims on this sacred path.

Table of Contents

Foreword

Have you ever been chased by a song? Have you ever, for no reason at all, found yourself suddenly humming a tune or singing a song?

Traditionally, American Indians had the custom of going alone on a four-day vision quest. Often, a vision for the rest of the Indian's life would be accompanied by a song. That song, called the "death song," gave courage in the face of difficulties. It would be sung as the Indian rode into battle.

Another interesting American-Indian custom was the "war dance." I always thought they were dancing to get angry enough to go into battle. Not so. The song and dance served to dispel any anger they held for the enemy and thus purified their intentions as they rode into battle.

When we look at the history of the book of Psalms, we find that in circa 1000 BC, when David was King, the Jews began to collect their folk songs. We now know the Holy Spirit inspired these songs. They were often written in praise of God, expressing many human emotions. The writers usually followed a pattern of expressing their oneness with their creator God, lamenting their feelings of separation and division, and ending with an experience of bonding and reunification with God and each other.

Around the year 500 BC, the psalms were placed into three separate volumes. Though our language does not accurately express the rhythm in which they were written, we find that certain psalms match the feelings and life experiences of our own day. These psalms become our own personal songs.

In this prayer book, *Ancient Psalms for Contemporary Pilgrims*, Jeanie Miley asks us to spend seven days praying one psalm, ending our prayers by contemplating questions that turn each psalm into our own song. Because of her unique gift, we can use this book to find psalms that lead us from darkness to light, from despair to hope, from doubt to faith, and from death to life. With a new vision, we can face life with courage and discover our own death song. And these songs begin to chase you.

Father Keith Hosey
Director of John 23 Center
Hartford City, Indiana

Preface

It was the middle of the night. I crept downstairs and found my Bible. Instinctively, I found Psalm 23, and while I didn't really need to read the words, I found comfort in seeing them on the well-marked page. How many times, through the years, had I returned to a practice I had learned as a young girl, finding solace and encouragement in the ancient affirmation of God's guidance!

The first time I attended an Ash Wednesday service, I had to move outside my own tradition. Instinctively, I knew that I needed the season of Lent. I needed that period of examination and confession, and so I joined my friends at Good Shepherd Episcopal Church in San Angelo, Texas, and prayed for the very first time the confession of David in Psalm 51, a psalm I had read literally hundreds of times. Suddenly, in the context of that Ash Wednesday service, the psalm had new meaning. I wrote the date in my Bible, and every time I read it, I revisit my first experience of praying that psalm of repentance.

"Praying the psalms" was a new idea for me, but one that resonated immediately with my own heart and mind. Out of my tradition, I knew how to speak to God easily and naturally in my own conversational forms. It was something else for me to enter into the words of another and make them mine, to let the heart's cry of another, albeit a biblical pray-er, become my own! It didn't take long, however, to discover that the grandeur of language of the psalms lifted my own thoughts and words to a new level. The beauty of the ancient text transformed my image of God and began to heal and enlarge my own heart.

On a crisp spring morning, I walked down a mountain road from the retreat center and entered the chapel of St. Benedict's Monastery in Snowmass, Colorado. Sitting in the silence in the simple room, I watched the rancher-monks enter, one by one, their simple capes thrown over their jeans and flannel shirts. Each went to his own chair and waited to begin the orderly, ancient practice of praying the psalms.

At the sounding of the bell, the monks rose silently, and so did we, retreatants and guests seated on either side of the chapel.

"Oh, Lord, come to my assistance," they chanted. "God, make haste to help me." Once again, they prayed the old, old words, joining their hearts and minds and intentions with thousands of pray-ers who, through the centuries, had found peace and power and presence in the words of the psalms.

How is it that these psalms have such power and potency that people have returned to them again and again for sustenance and comfort, renewal and release? What is it about them that makes men and women around the world willing to repeat them day after day, year after year? And why is there a renewed interest in these old, old songs today?

In my childhood, I learned a few entire psalms from memory, and also a few verses from several psalms, snatched from first one and then another of the ancient prayers. It was in my adulthood, however, when I began to teach from the book of Psalms in a weekday Bible class, that I began to discover the enormity of their scope and power. During my last yearlong teaching of these prayers I began to realize that immersing oneself in these prayers would change one's image of God. Indeed, in my work as a spiritual director, I often guided directees to various psalms when I realized that where they were stuck was in their view of God.

Just as the psalms could change one's image of God, they could also transform one's own self-image, bringing a person's view into conformity with God's view. The book of Psalms helps directees confess their own sin and heal difficult memories. Praying the psalms brings one's view of the world into alignment with God's view, and the relationship of people to the world is clarified in the psalms.

Within Psalms is found the full range of human emotion, and so praying the psalms provides a way for the pray-er to vent those strong emotions and heal afflicted feelings. The right psalms give strength and confidence; certain psalms give the courage to face hard situations or the boldness to trust God when life seems to indicate that God has vanished.

Praying the psalms must, as well, join us with the Spirit of Christ as he intercedes on our behalf. Surely, these are his prayers—the prayers he prayed as a young rabbi, the human Jesus, the incarnation of God.

Praying these psalms, we will be changed.

How to Use This Book

In the book of Psalms, we encounter a relationship between the transcendent, holy God and a fallible, ordinary human being so radical that the communication between the Holy Other and the pray-er bears examination. Perhaps by entering deeply into the psalms through prayer, lingering over the lines that "choose you" and taking into your heart the phrases that touch your wounded places, you may experience some of the same intimacy with God that Jesus experienced as he drew apart to pray. It is not hard to imagine that the wrestling of Jesus in Gethsemane mirrored the psalms of anguish and absence.

If intimacy is the sharing of one's failures and fears, and the revealing of feelings and longings of the heart with another, the book of Psalms reveals a revolutionary depth of communication and closeness with the Almighty, a closeness that could transform one's life from the inside out. Indeed, in the book of Psalms, the pray-er lays her heart wide open to God; nothing, it seems, is hidden as the psalmist runs the gamut of human emotion, pouring out prayers with the freedom and spontaneity of a child who has complete trust in the One to whom he prays. Anything is fair game for the psalmist's prayer life, and so it is for ours.

If a contemplative is one who experiences God in everything, the psalms reveal a true contemplative. It is hard to imagine an emotion of any person, ancient or contemporary, that is not addressed in the psalms.

Praying the psalms is an old and trusted custom. The practice and discipline must have great impact on the life of the one who prays, for the custom has been sustained through centuries and around the world. The book of Psalms provides the language for extolling and praising God, for giving thanks, for wrestling with the deepest and most disturbing human emotions—rage, terror, guilt, and inadequacy. The prayers find the pray-er in the depths of despair, lamenting the seeming absence of God, and then soaring to the heights of adoration and love for the God who is filled with love and mercy. Surely, anything that has been around as long as these psalms must be worthy of our attention.

In *Ancient Psalms for Contemporary Pilgrims*, the psalms are used as seeds for contemplation. The meditations for each psalm are intended not to explore doctrine or dogma, as important as those are. Instead, the meditations are designed to lead you to an encounter of the Living God and an experience of intimacy with the Holy Other.

Each week, you are invited to pray one psalm for seven days. Each day's meditation contains a thought or a question, evoked by the psalm itself, that is intended to move you into the recesses of your own heart to wrestle with your questions and yearnings in the presence of God and in the intent of the psalm. The meditations provide a way for us to "lean into our own questions" in the presence of God.

By entering thoughtfully into each day's meditation, you may find your concept of God changing from that of a faraway, distant, punitive deity to a present and available, loving and merciful presence. In focusing on the concept of God revealed in the psalms, you are invited to give up your god-concepts that are limited and limiting and perhaps, harmful. With a healing of the God-concept, your concept of your own life, your own place within creation, the purpose and meaning of your life, and your relationship with the world will change.

By nurturing this intimate communication with God that is patterned in the psalms, you will be able to open the depths of your own emotions to the One from whom nothing is hidden. Indeed, through the psalms, you may find the freedom to wrestle with your hardest questions in prayer. By exploring the issues of trust and obedience, gratitude and praise, forgiving and surrender in the language of the psalms and through the meditations, you will find a deep healing of emotion. Often, by praying the psalms, emotional knots of a lifetime are released and the prisons of one's own making are diminished or destroyed.

As in any spiritual practice, consistency and faithfulness to the practice have an increasingly significant impact on those who make themselves available for a breakthrough of God's grace. Choose a time and a place that works for you; return to this time and place each day. You may receive some gift of grace early in the process. Sometimes, it seems that God waits to see how serious we are about our practice.

To meditate on these Scriptures, turn the the words and the phrases over and over in your mind, as if you were chewing on them, determined to juice each one for every morsel of spiritual nourishment. The more you give to the process, the more the Psalms will give to you.

Each day, read the psalm for the week. Read it aloud and read it slowly. Read the psalm several times. Read it in more than one translation. You may want to memorize it. As you read, pay attention to the verses that resonate within your own heart. Sit in silence and let the words nestle in your mind and heart.

Read the day's meditation. Perhaps you will want to journal about the meditation or the question. Sit in silence for at least twenty minutes and let the One who draws near speak to you. Wait, as the psalmist said, on the Lord. God will speak.

If "nothing happens" in your meditation, carry the thoughts and the psalm with you throughout your day. Now and then, turn your mind toward the psalm. You will be surprised at the insight or understanding that will come to you, seemingly "out of the blue." When that happens, be sure to write it down!

Praying the psalms and meditating on them seems to be one of the ways God forms our faith. It is as if these ancient prayers are the potter's wheel, and the Holy Spirit, speaking the words of the psalms, is the Potter, shaping the willing and malleable life to the design for which he or she was made.

Expect to be changed by praying the psalms. Watch for amazing changes in the way you experience God and yourself and the world. You cannot determine the ways in which God will shape you, and you need not know how God will meet you or transform you; you only need to be willing to enter into the Mystery and consent to the work of the One who makes all things new.

A Prayer Book

The Invitation

Come into His Presence

In reading the psalms, it becomes clear that the dialogue between the one who prays and the sovereign Holy God is one of intimacy and familiarity. There is the sense that the one who prays does not invoke the presence of God so much as he or she becomes aware of it. The conversations of the psalms move naturally back and forth from God's words to the psalmist and the words of the psalmist back to God.

In contemplative praying, the pray-er comes to understand that all of creation is filled with the activity, purpose, and presence of God. We see the work of God in nature and in other people. We hear the voice of God in the voice of another person. We see God's handiwork in the middle of problems and crises. We experience God in worship and in acts of love. God is in all places, praying to his people, and God wants a response. The psalms give responses to the dynamic presence of God.

It is not we, then, who invite God to join us in our tasks and projects. It is God, the Creator of all things, who invites us to become so aware of his handiwork that we are able to move in step with God's activity and cooperate with it. It is God who has a plan for his handiwork; it is our privilege and opportunity to be co-creators and co participants with God to carry out God's plan. It is God who initiates; we follow.

True humility begins with an understanding that God starts the conversation with us. God knows how things work, and we are responsible to bring mind, heart, will, and willingness into alignment with God's idea.

Psalm 95

Around the world, and in many different languages, seekers after God gather in chapels and sitting rooms, monasteries and office spaces and pray this psalm, an ancient prayer that invites worshipers to stop for a moment and focus their attention on God.

For centuries, Psalm 95 has called people to prayer. Over time, this psalm has been the beginning point of worship, the announcement of a change of pace and a shift in focus. Those who have prayed this psalm for decades know that simply speaking of the first few words moves them into a deep state of prayer, centering them in the presence of God.

Nomadic people first prayed this psalm together. The words gathered them into a cohesive group from wherever they had been wandering and focused their attention on the Center of gravity that would ground them and guide them. This psalm invited early pilgrims to seek the one who had found them and to see with the eyes of their hearts the one whose eye was always on them.

Today, praying this psalm connects you with the Creator of the universe. It also connects you with fellow pilgrims around the world who take the time to stop and pray this old prayer anew. You do not pray alone, for you are part of the mystical Body of Christ.

In the communion of saints in your life, what individuals have helped shape your faith? Who encourages you today? What heroes of the faith would you call into your circle?

Psalm 95

DAY TWO

"Come, let us sing for joy to the Lord."

Millions of pray-ers begin their day with this invitatory psalm, joining their voices with others. Others pray alone in solitary cells or empty rooms.

Coming to prayer, each of us brings our many selves into the circle of God's love. Each of us brings the adult that we are, the child that we used to be, the parent that we carry around inside us. This psalm invites all of our various parts, known and unknown to our awareness, to prayer.

When I come to this prayer and when I focus my attention on the presence of God, I bring my strong self and my weak self to God. The part of me that is noble and high-minded comes, but I also bring that part of me that is self-seeking and base. The truth-teller comes, as well as the liar. The lover in me comes gladly; I have to pull the hater and the bigot into the circle. I bring the part of myself that is the prodigal into the presence of God, and the prideful, arrogant, resentful elder brother sometimes comes, but often holds back. Into this circle, I bring the part of me that is Mary, eager to anoint the feet of my Lord with my tears and my gift. Integrity demands that I also bring the Judas in me, that part of me I wish I didn't have, the part that will sell out. The beloved in me comes, like John, the beloved disciple, and I also bring the part of me that is Peter, my impulsive self, the part of me that denies Christ.

Picture your many selves coming into the presence of God, gathered around an altar. Call each part by name. Ask your disowned parts to come as well.

Psalm 95

So, where have you been, that you think you have to work so hard to find God? In what far country of the mind and heart have you been wandering?

How long has it been, anyway, since you realized you had forgotten to come to God? Did you even know you had neglected to take your concerns to him? Have you been too busy to notice that you didn't give God the time of day until you suddenly discovered that your inner well had run dry?

The reality is that God never moves. We do. God never takes his eye off us and he never lets us slip out of awareness, but we can go for days without remembering that there is nowhere we can go where God is not. We are never separated from God; only our perception makes us think that God is absent.

And so it is that we humans need a practice, a spiritual discipline, that provides the opportunity for us to turn our attention away from our own self-seeking, our own necessary tasks and troubles, our duties and responsibilities, important as they are, and focus our attention on the Source of life. Regularly and consistently, we need the routine of coming before God and singing for joy. We need to find our way back to the presence that never moves. We need to come before God intentionally and purposefully for our own spiritual nourishment as much as we need to eat and breathe and rest.

If spiritual disciplines are the ways and means of grace, what are you doing to keep your soul nourished?

Psalm 95

Those early pilgrims must have had the idea that coming before God, acknowledging him as the Source of all of creation, and singing praises to him and about him had value in their lives. They must have known, at some instinctual level, how dependent they were on God's guidance and care. Apparently, they were aware that it would be easy for them to drift away from this protecting and sustaining relationship, just as their forefathers had done.

There is something about reorienting our lives on a daily basis that keeps us remembering we are not God. Without that conscious awareness of the One who holds all things in his hands, it is easy to drift into forgetting God and playing God. Acknowledging the Sovereign One keeps our feet firmly planted on the ground. Remembering the Source protects us from the arrogance of thinking we are more than we are intended to be. Speaking the truth about the order of things in the presence of others has a way of keeping humility alive.

God seems to work best through people who know who they are and who they aren't. God has bestowed great dignity and worth on human lives. God has given great power to human beings. The world seems to run best, however, when humans remember who is in charge and who is not.

Is there some area of your life in which you are attempting to play God? What would it cost you to give it up and play your own part?

Psalm 95

Surely, in that group of early pilgrims, somebody came to worship in a foul mood! Surely, here and there was a doubter, a resistor, a rebel, or a coward. With so many people, somebody had to have a cold or a hangover, and there had to have been someone in the group with a sour temperament. Among the most pious of the bunch, surely somebody wasn't in the mood to come before the Lord with music and thanksgiving!

So what are we to do when we are having a difficult day or get bad news right before worship? How can we sing praises with a heavy heart or a burdened mind? What happens when we can't think of a single reason for thanksgiving, even if we are blessed beyond measure?

There is something mysterious and powerful about choosing to put aside your troubles and heartaches and focus on the power and presence of God. Something happens inside the cold heart or the closed mind with the intentional choosing of worship.

There are times when we don't feel like praising God. In fact, there may be long, hard seasons when worship is dry and prayer is boring. Still, we come before the Lord in faith. We tell the truth about how we feel, but we keep on coming. We keep on doing what we know will make a difference, and one day, the feelings catch up and we sing, once again, with joy.

What do you feel when you don't feel the joy of the Lord?

Psalm 95

Alcoholics and other folks who work through the Twelve Steps of Alcoholics Anonymous testify to the power of stating your addiction regularly and publicly. Sobriety—emotional, financial, sexual, or physical—depends on remembering that the tendency to "slip" is always present. To forget your character defect, your tendency to choose darkness over light, is to flirt with disaster. To ignore the reality of the tendency of the self-will to run riot is to create the possibility of losing one's way and returning to addictive behaviors.

The children of Israel knew the stories of their forefathers, and they knew the bitter results of rebellion against God. They knew the logical consequences of hard hearts and stiff necks, of forgetting the loving care and reliable guidance of God. They had to remind themselves of what could happen if they forgot the way of life. They needed to remember, regularly and consistently, outsold and in public, that choosing death over life, darkness over light, rebellion over cooperation was always a possibility. They needed to remember that their very lives depended on their keeping first things first.

Do you know what kinds of things—people, places, events—get you off track and off your program of life and worship? Are you aware of your personal tendencies to rebel and go your own way? What is your personal far country? What can you do to stay centered and grounded in God?

Psalm 95

The early pilgrims had their gods, those idols they looked to for meaning and purpose, guidance and protection. They needed to declare that the One True God was the only God that mattered, the only One who could really protect them. It wasn't that God needed to hear them say that he was the great God, above all gods, for his sake. The *people* needed to say it; they needed to affirm the great God.

We, too, have our gods. In spite of our sophistication and education, we make idols of things and processes. We make our children into gods, and we ask our spouses and our religious leaders to be gods for us. We put education, technology, medicine, and commerce on a pedestal, offering sacrifices of time and money to appease them. We attempt to make nations into god, and we ask the corporation or our institutions to carry that projection. Some of us even make the church or the denomination into an idol, demanding that it do for us what it cannot do.

Sometimes, we give lip service to God, blithely going through life oblivious to the fact that we really do worship things and people. We forget that whenever we turn someone or something into an idol, we will either destroy it or it will destroy us. Declaring God as God, giving God our ultimate worth, is the way to keep the order of creation in its proper alignment and perspective. The first commandment is, after all, for our benefit. Loving God first and most makes the world run right.

Do you know what your gods are? How do you feel about firing them and letting the great God take first place in your affections? What would that cost you?

Psalm 23:1

DAY ONE

"The Lord is my shepherd."

Is that well-loved statement an affirmation, a statement of faith? Is it a confidence-builder, an anchor brought forth in rough times? Or is it a reminder when we forget Who is in charge of the world?

Perhaps we pray those ancient words for different reasons at various times. Perhaps it is most powerful when the opening verse of what is likely the most famous and most memorized psalm is a statement of our choosing. In this psalm, we choose God, the Good Shepherd, as our shepherd.

In your imagination, "see" the various people to whom you have given yourself, hoping that each would lead you to a place of security and solace. Picture, in your mind's eye, the heroes you have installed in your life, emulating their choices or beliefs. See all of those lesser gods in a lineup, parading across the screen of your memory, ordinary mortals whom you have elevated to positions of power and influence in your life.

With your mental paintbrush, picture a beautiful, lush meadow. See the green grass and the blue sky overhead. Hear the song of the birds. Inhale deeply; fill your lungs with clean, pure air. Feel the gentle brush of wind on your face. Imagine this as a place of perfect peace and security. Now, imagine yourself standing before the One who really can lead you to the places where you are intended to be. See the Good Shepherd standing before you in that meadow. This is the One who has only your best welfare in mind. Picture the Good Shepherd looking at you with unconditional love and acceptance.

Return to this mental picture throughout the day. What feelings does it evoke?

Psalm 23:2-3a

Return, in your imagination, to the setting of yesterday's meditation. Choose to use all of your senses to picture the encounter between yourself and the Good Shepherd.

Let this image be the "seed for contemplation" throughout the day. Return to it at regular intervals, taking a few seconds to stop whatever you are doing. Inhale deeply and exhale fully, letting yourself pause in the presence of the Good Shepherd. Choose the Good Shepherd as the One you will trust for your well-being.

For a while, hold only the picture in your mind's eye. Stay with that moment of meeting, using all of your five senses to experience being in the presence of the Good Shepherd. Smell the fresh aromas and hear the sounds of nature. Feel the gentle sun, warming your face. Taste the cool water. See the love of the Shepherd for you.

As you breathe in, imagine peace and serenity filling up the inner spaces of your mind and heart. Choose the Good Shepherd as your shepherd.

Repeat the words of these verses either silently or aloud, picturing the green of the pastures. Hear the gentle lapping of quiet waters.

Know that merely being in the presence of the Good Shepherd has restorative powers. Know that there is nowhere you can go where this presence is not there. Remember that the Good Shepherd knows exactly how you need to be restored. That is his job. Your job is simply to turn your attention toward that presence.

William Blake said that the senses "are the inlets to the soul." Use all of your senses to create an encounter with the One who is always present with you.

Psalm 23:3b

For some of us, it is hard to believe that merely practicing being in the presence of God every day will make a difference in the circumstances of our lives. We are conditioned to earn our rewards and strive for God's favor. We are programmed to seek results and measure outcomes, so programmed that we transfer that "works" mentality into our life with God. We look outside for guidance, not realizing that true guidance flows from our resting in the heart of God.

Through the centuries, seekers have discovered power in the daily practice of meditation. It is not, however, the power that ego can seize and use for its own purposes. Instead, it is the power of being right with God and with the purpose of one's own life.

Ego craves security and homeostasis. The purpose of God, however, written into each person, has little concern with the ego's happiness or security. On the other hand, God, who dwells within, is at work in all things, attempting to guide us back to authentic righteousness, a right relationship with God and with one's own purpose.

Devise a plan that fits your lifestyle, but stretch yourself a little. Find a time, twice a day, and picture yourself in the presence of God. Try for twenty minutes, morning and night. Give yourself to the discipline of meditation, and see if the practice doesn't reveal to you that the Good Shepherd will bring you back from the places you've been wandering to the place you're meant to be, right in the heart of God. He will guide you to the only pasture that is truly safe, and from there, to the only places you need to go.

Will you commit to this discipline for thirty days? Will you rest in the presence of God?

Psalm 23:4

DAY FOUR

In our rational, materialistic world, the rule is, "I'll believe it when I see it."

A spiritual perspective, however, says, "I'll see it when I believe."

It's a risk, choosing to let the Good Shepherd be the one on whom you place your trust for your whole life. It is certainly a risk to believe that using your imagination to picture yourself in the presence of that Good Shepherd can make a difference in the way you live your life at work and at home.

The effects of the simple, yet profound practice of meditation are often seen best in the way the meditator responds to the events of life. In the dull, mundane, and ordinary events of life, the one who is in relationship with the Good Shepherd has an attitude of joy. In the challenges of everyday life, meditators seem to have access to internal resources of creativity that non-meditators look for in the outer world.

It is in the dark valleys of life, however, that those who are on familiar terms with the Good Shepherd most experience the effects of a vibrant, dynamic love-relationship with the one who comforts and sustains. It isn't that the pain of suffering is taken away. Indeed, all humans experience pain and suffering.

It is that a consistent, daily choice to be with the Good Shepherd somehow gives a person assurance and comfort. One who knows the Good Shepherd, through daily encounters and consistent communication, trusts in him through the valley and out of it.

Today, take the risk to believe that God is with you in the valleys of life. Imagine what that means for you. Choose to trust that what has worked for others will work for you.

Psalm 23:5a

There is a sequence in this psalm, and when you begin to live it in the ordinary experiences of everyday life, you begin to live with a different worldview and a different spirit. Choosing to live this psalm as a dynamic prayer breathed throughout the day is choosing to live with confidence. In many ways, Psalm 23 has the same point as John 15—that when you live in the natural relationship with God, you have what you need to do what you are meant to do. Psalm 23 is a treatment plan that works.

Moving into the silence and into the world of your imagination, take time to re-create the visual image of standing before the Good Shepherd. Choose to rest in that presence, both for specific moments set aside during the day and internally as you go about your various responsibilities. Choose to hold the connection between your own self and God by picturing yourself with God. Risk believing that this is the way to serenity and peace.

Move your focus to a banquet table, a symbol of God's provisions. Affirm that in this holy rest, the choice to live surrendered to God, everything you need is provided. Choosing to be with the Good Shepherd is choosing sustenance and strength.

Move your focus deeper into your own life and identify the enemies that wreak havoc with your inner life and your outer world. Name the ways that fear and insecurity, hate and anger, guilt and shame debilitate you. Admit those enemies. Confess them to God, and then affirm again that God's presence is sufficient for meeting those forces that would defeat and discourage you.

If you are letting your enemies lead you, why not choose the Good Shepherd instead?

Psalm 23:5b

Do you wonder what to do with your to-do list? Do you debate which priority to meet first? How do you choose what you will do with your talents and gifts? Do you want to do something, to live out your own unique vocation and call, but instead hide in fear and doubt? Are you overwhelmed with the tasks that lie before you, feeling inadequate or ineffective in the face of them?

Imagine yourself spending time in the presence of the Good Shepherd. Choose to imagine yourself being watched over and provided for by him. Can you sense how it would feel to be at ease, confident that you are being led by one with your best welfare in mind? Imagine that you have what you need to do what you must do.

In your mind's eye, hold that vision of yourself with the Good Shepherd while you scan the tasks that beckon to you. Which ones are really yours? Which ones are meant for you to do? What belongs to you, and what belongs to someone else? What is your responsibility, and what is not? Which tasks are in harmony with the intent of the Good Shepherd for you? Which ones satisfy ego? Which ones make your heart sing?

Choosing time with God aligns God's purpose with your choices for how you will use your resources. Meditating on the presence of God provides clarity of thought and focus. Staying connected with the One who knows how things are supposed to be gives good, orderly direction from within. It creates the possibility for God to provide an overflow of whatever resource is needed for the task.

And that is an anointing from the overflowing bounty of God.

Do you trust God to give you what you need for the task at hand? If not, why not?

Psalm 23:6

As you move into the silence for today, take some time to breathe deeply, as if you were out in the fresh air with a real shepherd. Recreate that pastoral setting. Imagine how it would be to feel at ease and at rest, in the presence of the Good Shepherd.

Review your day. Call to mind the things that worry you. Bring to the forefront of your mind the issues that you can't seem to resolve or solve. Don't engage with them; instead, just observe them as if they were part of the landscape.

In the silence, hold each concern in your mind, as if you were holding it before God. Tell God your feelings about that concern. Speak the unvarnished truth with boldness. Hold nothing back. God knows it all, anyway, so you might as well bring it into full consciousness.

As you remain in stillness, affirm that God's goodness and love are pursuing you, even into this present moment or present difficulty. Recall the spiritual principle that God is at work in all things, attempting to bring about wholeness.

Remember: the reason you can affirm this is that you are choosing to "dwell in the house of the Lord forever." You are choosing, breath by breath and day by day, to live in the presence of the Good Shepherd, led and guided, sustained and nurtured by his care.

Choose it again and again. Affirm it over and over. Make it your lifestyle to live in the house of the Lord. Be who God designed you to be, and let God be who God is to you. It's the natural, intended way to live. It isn't your reward; it is the way.

What are the things that keep you from the life you are meant to live? What are you going to do about those things?

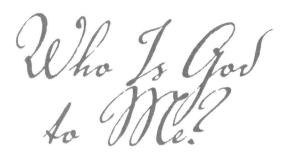

Healing the God-image

"Tell me about the God you don't believe in, for I probably don't believe in that God, either." I often say this to people who announce that they cannot believe in God.

"You need to fire that God and get a new one!" I sometimes say this to people living with an image of God that beats them up and keeps them feeling defeated and discouraged.

Through the years, I have come to see that the God-concept we carry is the most important concept we have. Who we believe God to be shapes our view of the world, our view of ourselves, and our view of how things work together—or don't!—in the daily interchanges between people. Our view of God affects our prayer life, our work life, our love life, and our money life.

The problem is that our God-image is formed in the earliest stages of development, and that image is based on the earliest caregivers or authority figures. An infant begins to learn at her first breath if the caregiver is attentive, responsive, responsible, consistent, loving, and nurturing, or if the caregiver is self-absorbed, neglectful, inattentive, withholding, or cruel. The personality of the earliest caregiver often transfers to a child's image of God.

Praying the psalms has the potential for healing or repairing the God-image. Praying the psalms and concentrating on the life-giving and life-supporting attributes of God can reprogram the mind and the heart, reorienting the pray-er around truth instead of lies about who God is and how God wants to be in relationship with us. How you see God may or may not be how God is. Are you willing to change your view?

Psalm 27:1-3

Remember a time when you watched a small child see the lights of a Christmas tree for the first time. Imagine being that child.

Bring to your conscious mind the vision of sunlight playing on the ocean or moonlight dancing in the waves. Recall the fascination with the way water reflects light.

Re-create a time when you came from darkness into a brightly lighted room. Remember how you blinked your eyes while they became accustomed to the light.

Remember a time when a "lightbulb" went off in your head, a time when insight broke through your present understanding, illuminating the darkness of confusion or doubt and helping you to see something in your life more clearly.

Jesus said that he was "the light of the world." The psalmist declares that the Lord is his light. What does that mean for you today, that God is Light? What does it mean for you to be in the presence of Light? How does being in the Light give guidance?

Imagine that you are sitting "in the Light," in the presence of God. Imagine that Light as a healing presence, penetrating the darkness of what is not well within you. Imagine the Light exposing the darkness of your mind and heart.

What would it be like for you to walk in the Light, day by day? How would your life be different from the way it is now? Given a choice, would you prefer to stay in darkness or walk in the Light of the presence of God?

If God is Light, what do you have to do to walk in the Light? What are the risks? What are the dangers of not walking in the Light?

Psalm 27:1-3

As you begin your time of reflection and silence today, recall the affirmation of the psalmist: The Lord is my light. Remember the image of yourself being in the Light of God. Imagine yourself returning to that Light day after day, choice by choice.

The psalmist declares, as well, that the Lord is salvation, or wholeness. Is it possible that being in the Light makes us become whole? Is it possible that consciously choosing to be people of the Light brings the broken parts of ourselves back together? Can it be that simple?

If God is Love, then being with God (or, more accurately, being aware of being with God) is a way of allowing the enlightening and healing activity of God to permeate your life in such a way that you are transformed from the inside out. Being with God, who is Love, allows the Divine Therapist to beam a healing ray into the emotional knots of your heart. It allows that healing Love to illuminate the dark corners of your mind, exposing the lies you tell yourself that keep you in prisons of your own making. That process of salvation—of being made whole—is accomplished as you surrender to the One who is Love.

It's a risky venture, spending time with Love. God might change your mind and change your life. That Lover of your soul just might really heal a part of you that you use as a crutch. God might turn your old habits upside down and take away the attachments that no longer serve you. Live the truth, choice by choice.

Affirm that God is your light and your salvation over and over until you believe it. Dare to accept the light and the salvation. Dare to live it. Dare to live in Love.

Psalm 27:1-3

If you can bear it, take some time to make two lists of your greatest fears. List those things in the outer world that scare you. List those demons in your inner world, those secret fears that only you know about. Which are worse, those on the outside or those you carry around with you?

Imagine what it would be to sit in the presence of God with your lists. What if you could hold each item on your list up to the Light of God and get God's point of view on each thing you fear? Can you see each of those things you fear as the things that keep you from wholeness? Where are the various places—activities, addictions, people—you have run to, trying to get away from the things you fear?

As you return to the silence, breathe deeply, exhaling those things that you fear, one by one. As you inhale, affirm who God is: Light, Salvation, Strength.

Dare to imagine that being with God is the answer to your deepest fears. Picture how your life might be if you could move your attention away from the thing that you think is causing your pain and place your attention in the presence of God. What if, instead of hiding out in the dark cave of your fear, you chose to walk boldly in the presence of God, claiming that presence as the real stronghold for your life?

There is no safety in worry. There is no peace in obsessing about your enemies. There is no serenity in engaging with your anxiety and feeding your fears. You can acknowledge them and call them what they are, but then you can return to the real safety of the presence of God. There is no place you can go where God is not.

Wake up to the reality of the abiding presence of God. Count on it. Look for it.

Psalm 27:4-6

DAY FOUR

The psalmist says he has one request, and that is to dwell in the house of the Lord forever. Jesus says, "Abide in me, and I will abide with you" (John 15).

In the silence, imagine that you could go back to that moment when God created humankind. Imagine, if you can, that you could see inside the mind of God as the Creator began to put into humankind the qualities and tendencies of humanness. Imagine the Creator giving humans desires and yearnings, longings and needs, none of which can be seen on an x-ray machine.

Think about all of your longings. Think about what you wanted when you were a child, an adolescent, a young adult. What yearnings motivated you at each stage of your development? What hungers needed to be fed?

Return in your imagination to that moment of your conception. In that sacred moment, you were created with a hunger to know God. The need to dwell with God was placed within you, creating a vacuum that only the presence of God can fill.

It's a risk to believe that the One whom you seek is seeking you and that your hunger can be filled by spending time in solitude and silence each day, focusing on the presence of God within you. As you dare to take that risk, however, you will discover that God will meet you there, in intimacy. In the simple act of the humility of abiding, you will find protection and deliverance. God will meet you at the point of your need. At the place of your inadequacy, the adequacy of God will find you.

How much do you really want to dwell in the house of the Lord? However much you want God, God wants you even more.

35

Psalm 27:4-6

Sometimes, events play out in such a way that God has clearly intervened. At other times, it seems that God helps those who help themselves. All humans have to grapple with the challenge of knowing which things can be changed and which ones must be accepted. There are those situations in life from which we want to be rescued, in whatever way possible. We beg God to get us out of some things and into others. Mostly, we want quick fixes and instant answers.

Much of life, however, is spent in process. God's deliverance happens most often in stages and as we cooperate with the dynamic, active power of God amid our difficulties. The purpose of meditation or of contemplative prayer, then, is not to hide from problems but to retreat for a time in order to gain the resources we need to deal with the challenges and difficulties of everyday life. Prayer is not an escape but a voluntary resting in order to gain strength and guidance.

In the silence, imagine yourself in the safety of God's presence, a presence so real that you feel it as ultimate security. Feel yourself fully grounded in the presence, as if "set upon a rock." Imagine yourself lifting your head in confidence and faith, able to sing amid difficulty, giving praise and thanks to God.

Hold this picture of yourself. In this safe place, the Light of God fills you with whatever you need to do what challenges you. In this presence, you are being equipped to face your dangers as opportunities. The Light will show you the next step to take. After that, you'll see the next step and then the next one.

Are you willing to take the next step, even without seeing the whole picture?

Psalm 27:7-12

Imagine yourself standing before God, in whatever way you choose. The only condition is that you remember that this presence is Light and Salvation, Strength and Love.

Let your mind scan your history for a list of all the ways you have tried to fix yourself. Remember the things you have done to try to gain serenity and peace. Look at your accomplishments, achievements, and acquisitions as you are in the Light. Did any of them fill the hole in your soul? Is there anything outside yourself that satisfied your deepest longings?

As you stand before this holy presence, imagine that God reminds you that he is, after all, the One who created you with the desire to seek him. It is he who put within you the impulse for relationship with the Creator. It is God, the One you seek, who seeks you!

Imagine yourself saying to God, "This seeking you is your idea, and since it is your idea, I can count on you to make it happen."

Is it possible that God is in the middle of your hardest questions, beckoning you toward the answers? Is it possible that God is in the middle of your most tangled problems, showing you the straight path? Can it be that God is in the middle of your character defect, your greatest failure, your deepest agony, your darkest night, inviting you into his heart? Will you accept that the first thing to do in any situation is to seek God?

Will you dare to look into the darkness to see the Light? Will you seek God anywhere?

Psalm 27:13-14

In the silence of today, take a look at the places of your impatience. Look at the times when you wait to see what everyone else will do, keeping your focus on fallible human beings instead of waiting for God to move.

Waiting on God is not passivity or inaction. It is not being irresponsible or letting things go. Waiting on God is not about living in a bunker, looking through the cracks of the wall to see what others are doing.

Waiting on God is about full participation in life. It is about engaging with what is, but in such a way that God has room to work. Waiting on God is about living in the confidence of the One who works all things for good. It is letting go into the plans and processes of God, allowing things to unfold in the way that brings healing and wholeness to one's own life and that of others. Waiting on God is like waiting for spring to come, though you cannot see the life force for winter's stillness. It is like waiting for a baby to be formed, though you cannot see what is shaped in the womb.

Today, practice waiting on God by being still in the silence. Be willing to have nothing take place. Affirm that God is at work in the recesses of your innermost heart, whether you can feel it or see evidence of it. Simply wait, one breath at a time.

As you wait, you will come to know the One who is always at work, in all things, bringing about his purposes. As you wait in the silence, you will come to hear the One who sings (Zephaniah 3:17). And then you will come to know that that is enough.

What keeps you from waiting on God? In what area do you most need to wait on him?

Psalm 63:1

According to some scholars, this psalm/prayer was written by David when he was in the Desert of Judah. "Desert," of course, is symbolic of a dry and barren place. Desert conjures images of vast stretches of sand where nothing blooms. For centuries, the term "desert experience" has been used to indicate a time of spiritual emptiness, necessary for the development of stout faith.

Today, as you enter the silence and focus on the idea of desert, let your mind summon the great cloud of witnesses who have gone before you into a desert experience. Think of the spiritual giants of history who have endured times of deep soul dryness and imagine them gathered around you.

Hear David's affirmation, "Oh, God, you are my God." Repeat it to yourself several times. Say it slowly as you breath deeply. Hear the intimacy with which David approaches the Holy Other.

Intimacy with God is an affirmation that you have a "place to go" where God is with you. Recall words from the psalms that describe that place: shelter, resting place, sanctuary, shadow of his wings. God is rock, fortress, and rest.

Note, however, that you go to that "place" internally. It is the "prayer closet" that Jesus described. It is an inner experience intended to give you what you need. It is not, however, a hideout or an escape hatch.

Imagine a God so mysterious that you can go to him and find what you need.

What helps you "go to" God? What keeps you from going?

Psalm 63:1

As you enter into the silence, let yourself remember a time when you were desperately thirsty or hungry. If you don't have the incident in your memory bank, imagine hunger and thirst so great that you would do almost anything for food and drink.

Moving deeper into your awareness, recall a time when you wanted to know God with all of your heart. Either remember or imagine what it was like to want to know God so much that you would do anything to experience the presence of the Living God. It may be that the time was when you had come to the end of your intellectual wonderings and nothing satisfied that gnawing hunger in your heart. The time may have come in the midst of the dark night of the soul, when you felt as if God had abandoned you.

As you hold this memory of longing in your attention, remember the writer of Psalm 63. Connect with his experience of longing for God, and join the ranks of millions of seekers who have sat where you are, wanting to know God.

Imagine the location of that longing in your body. Where do you feel it most? It is a dull ache or a sharp pain? Do you experience longing for God as a hunger for something to fill the hole in your soul? Or are you so full of other things that there is no room for the longing? Could it be that you numb the longing, afraid to feel the depth of it? Do you fear that the One you seek will not let you find him?

Remember that the ability to seek God is evidence that God has found you. The One you seek is seeking you. The Seeking God, the One you want, wants you.

What gods have you been seeking? What do they do for you? What can the One True God do for you? Will you seek him today?

Psalm 63:3, 6

DAY THREE

On this day, recall times in the past when you have experienced God. Go back to childhood and move forward, noting those moments when grace broke through your experience and touched you in a way that you have never forgotten.

Memory is both gift and burden. It allows us to go back in time and re-create a meaningful moment. We can remember the past to connect with God's activity in that time and place, but we cannot ever return it.

Sometimes, in our life with God, we want to hold on to the past or re-create that moment in the present. The experiences of the past can give us confidence that the One who acted in that moment in history is also able and willing to break into the present moment in a new and fresh way. We must be good stewards of our memories.

Move deeply into your silence. As you inhale, imagine yourself breathing in the provision of God for this moment. As you exhale, imagine yourself letting go of the past. As good or rich or meaningful as it was, let it go. You can remember what God did in the past, but you cannot experience God in the past. You can hope for what God might do in the future, but you cannot experience God in the future. The only moment in which you can experience God is right now. The presence is in the present, and the power of God is in this place, where you are and in this time.

Are you willing to be fully present where you are? Are you willing to be with God now?

Psalm 63

DAY FOUR

In the end, only love keeps us seeking and choosing God. It is God's love, and not judgment, that somehow comes alive in the depths of our hearts, quickening memory and igniting desire to know and feel and live in that love relationship once again.

For a few moments, sit in the silence and simply love God. For a few minutes, imagine yourself in God's presence, extending love toward God. Breathe in God's love for you; breathe out your love for God. Don't do anything; just sit there, loving God.

If you choose, remember former times when you felt God's love for you. Bring those experiences into the center of your mind and recall what it was like to be loved unconditionally. Choose to feel the emotions that accompany this kind of experience.

If you have never felt that love from God or love for God, imagine what it would be to have that experience. Let the depth of your hunger for God be the sign of how much God wants to fill that emptiness with love.

Try an experiment. As you move from this time of meditation, take with you these words from 1 John 4: "God is love." Take on the open-minded and open-hearted attitude of a child and risk believing God truly is love. Repeat the verse as a prayer and affirmation of what is true. Repeat it as a choice you are making, a choice to receive God's love for you right now.

See how consistently you can hold that thought—"God is love"—in your daily life. After all, God wants you to know his name.

What difference does it make to know God as Love? as the Beloved? as Lover?

Psalm 63

On my desk sits a brass paperweight shaped like the Hebrew symbol for "life." It is a vital, dynamic symbol for me of God, who is Life.

God is the life force, coursing through the world, giving life to his creation. God is the creative spark that inspires creativity and productivity. He is the force that creates life and new life, bringing forth resurrection from what seems to be dead or lost. God is alive, and God is alive in us!

As you move into the period of stillness with God, let your mind be calm and quiet. Recall the image of the vine and the branches. Feel the deep intimacy of that connection and then transfer the image to your own life with God.

Scan your life and let the Spirit of God reveal to you where the energy of life is blocked. See what dreams have been dammed up and what emotions are stuck. Where is your creativity hitting the wall? What is blocking the flow of God's love from his heart into yours? What choices of your everyday routine are life-giving? What choices make you feel dead or lifeless?

If your life with God is stuck, it is likely that other relationships will be stuck. If your energy is down, it is likely that you have lost the connection with the Life-giver.

In this quiet, picture the Life-giver moving into those stuck places and beginning to unblock the flow of life. Imagine what your life would be if God's Life flowed, unhindered, into every part of your inner world and your outer world?

Breathe in and imagine that God is breathing new life into your being.

Fear is a common barrier to the flow of love. Where is it at work in your life?

Psalm 63

Here it is, right here in the Old Testament. For those who have eyes to see and the willingness to know, the character sketch of a loving God fills this part of Holy Scripture.

Scan Psalm 63 and write the character sketch of God. Here is the God who watches over you, the shelter who will protect and provide for you.

Here is the God who satisfies the longings of the soul with love and with the kind of power that equips.

Here is the God who inspires the seeking by nudging us through our longings and our intuitive hunches that somehow make us know God is the Source of the nourishment we need.

Take these thoughts about God and ponder them in the silence. Choose to focus on the image of God revealed in this psalm. Let these big ideas about God sink from your head into your heart, and imagine yourself resting fully in the presence of this God, the God whose love is better than life.

We are anthropomorphic beings. We make God into our image all the time. Often, our image of God is more like the image of a parent or an early authority figure. What would it take for you to change your image of God? If someone told you that your image of God could change by daily meditation on the loving presence of God, and that your whole life would change as a result, would you make the commitment to meditation?

Can you accept that such a simple discipline could have such a profound result?

Psalms 62 and 63

A bird flies in air. A fish swims in water. We live in God. God is our natural habitat, the place where we are. God is the place where we are intended to dwell. Meditating on the presence of God is the way that leads us to that long-lost home. Meditating is abiding, dwelling, or resting in the presence of God.

The only thing that separates us from God is that which we use to block out the consciousness of God's presence within. It may be an afflictive feeling that keeps you from knowing the kingdom of God within you. It may be a limited or limiting belief about God. It may be your own refusal to see what is right there within you.

As you read these psalms, take a risk and dare to believe that God is near and that God is here for you. Make a list of all that is provided in the safe shelter of intimacy with God. What is here for you, right now, given by the great provider God?

Moving into the silence and stillness, focus on your breathing. As you breathe in, repeat the spiritual blessing that you need most on this particular day. Pause and wonder if that is what you really need or if it is what your ego thinks you need.

As you breathe out, repeat the barrier that keeps you from receiving the blessing of God. It may be an afflictive emotion such as fear or guilt, shame or insecurity, hate or anger. It may be a problem so big that it takes up all the room in your mind and heart. It may be something you want more than you want the presence of God. Let your exhalation be a confession of this barrier to God. Then, sit in the silence and dare to wonder if that really is the barrier, or if there is something deeper.

Breathe in the blessing of God. Breathe out the barrier. Dare to believe.

Psalm 107:1

For today, begin your period of silence by recalling the people who have gone before you in the faith journey. Think of the people throughout history who have sought God in various ways. Remind yourself of the prayers of the people of God, prayers offered in many languages. In your imagination, place yourself with those people.

Move from that large thought to a more personal one. Bring your focus to your own journey and your own intimate, personal love relationship with God. Think of the ways God has drawn near to you. Recall the times when you have sought the One who seeks you.

As you sit in the silence, let your mind hold the first verse Psalm 107. Speak it silently or gently. "Give thanks to the LORD, for he is good; his love endures forever."

As you let your mind rest there, allow the idea that God is good hold center stage in your attention. Focus on that goodness. Imagine what it means for your personal life and for the community of faith.

If you were to define the goodness of God, what would you say? How is it different from the goodness of your particular culture? Is "goodness" the same as "following the rules"?

Where do you see evidence of God's goodness in your life? Where do you see it at work in difficulties? What about in nature? Where has that goodness surprised you? And where are you blocking that goodness from flowing through you?

Imagine yourself as the recipient of the goodness of God. Imagine that your mind and heart are open to God's goodness all during this day. Record the evidence.

Psalm 107:1b, 8a, 15a, 21a, 31a

DAY TWO

At the beginning of today's meditation, take a mental look at your day's activities. See in your mind's eye the challenges you must meet. Hold your attention on those tasks that are dull and boring. If there is something ahead that you dread, see it, too.

Holding your attention on those tasks that lie before you, breathe deeply and affirm that in the midst of each one, God's love endures forever.

You don't have to believe it. With the psalmist, simply affirm God's enduring love. Choose to live in the middle of your own life with that conciseness of God's enduring love. You don't have to see evidence of it. Walk in faith onto an edge where you have never been and dare to risk that God's love really is enduring. You don't have to feel it, either. Confess your own fears and doubts. Bring into the light what lurks in the darkness, trying to scare you away from love. God's love is strong enough to stand against the most severe test. Enduring Love is who God is.

Let the implications of this love that never ends, never gives up, and never lets you down to permeate your mind and heart. Imagine it settling down deep into your heart, a place where it cannot be taken away from you.

Stay in that space of God's enduring love for as long as you need. Write the choice on a card to carry with you. Pause throughout the day and choose it again. Choose to believe in the God whose love never fails, never gives up, never gets tired, never ebbs, and never turns away. Choose the God whose name is Love, breath by breath.

If you knew nothing else about God, would it be enough to know that God is Love? Does anything else you know about God compare with Love?

Psalm 107:2-9

You don't have to wait until you get to the New Testament to know God as Redeemer. From the beginning, the God of the Old Testament is the One who buys us back. God is the One who created us with free will, but who also goes looking for us to bring us back to the where we need to be.

As you think back on your life, recall the various "desert wastelands" in which you have wandered. It's easy to account for the obvious wastelands of addiction and perversion. Most of us, however, wander into the more subtle desert experiences that are often invisible to the outer world.

Perhaps you wandered into a negative mind-set and are living with a godless worldview. You may know the pain of practical atheism that allows you to carry on all of the religious rituals, but with an unbelieving wasteland heart. You may know the desert wasteland of trying too hard, of seeking meaning where there is no meaning. You may be wallowing in ingratitude or in doubts that take you nowhere you really want to be. Perhaps you have simply lost your passion and your wonder. God is the One who brings you back home.

Now, imagine what it would be for the Redeemer to come for you, perhaps in response to your plea for mercy. Can you imagine that your longing is a plea for the One who nourishes to come and get you, even if you have wandered away from where you know you need to be? Visualize, in your mind's eye, the wonder of being brought back home. It is, after all, evidence of God's love that you even know you have wandered away.

What will it take for you to take God's hand and let him lead you back home?

Psalm 107:10-16

An old story tells of a child visiting Carlsbad Caverns. When the guide turned out the lights in the cavern and the child experienced the deepest dark she'd ever known, she began to weep. "Don't worry, little sister," her big brother said to her. "I know the one who knows how to turn on the lights."

Today, as you close your eyes and enter into the silence, imagine the darkest darkness you have ever experienced. Try to feel the anguish of spiritual darkness, a darkness that seems endless.

Picture yourself imprisoned in a dungeon. Imagine the depth of that darkness. Ponder the terrible state of spiritual darkness, of prejudice, hate, and terror.

After you have imagined that state of dark imprisonment, picture the Redeemer coming to turn on the lights. Imagine God's coming to you, wherever you are, and releasing you from bondage! God is the Great Liberator!

Imagine the chains of slavery to a system that no longer "works" being broken. Picture being set free from the chains of addiction or worry or fear. See God bringing you out of the dungeon of despair, freeing you from hopelessness and helplessness into the light of God's presence.

As you sit in the silence, choose to surrender to the unfailing love of God and be set free. Breathe out all that oppresses you and darkens your world. Breathe in the healing, liberating love of the Redeemer.

Give thanks for the reality that while you may not be able to see what is happening, you know that God intends to buy you back and set you free.

Psalm 107:17–22

There's the foolish way of outright rebellion, the trap you create when you look into the face of something you know you shouldn't do, and you do it anyway.

There's another foolish way, the way of wandering off the good path by being negligent or foolhardy, by thinking the rules that apply to everyone else don't apply to you.

For today, imagine a God who is able to tolerate our foolishness and our rebelliousness, a God who understands that with free will, sometimes we choose well and sometimes we don't. This is a God who allows us the consequences of our choices, but who, with our outcry for deliverance, will accommodate himself to come and get us.

Perhaps God is coming to you through the trumpet sound of a major crisis. This time, he may approach you through the dull ache of an ongoing depression. God speaks, beckoning to us in physical symptoms and our dreams. Often, God is right in the middle of a character defect, a failure, a heartbreak, wooing us back to the place we need to be.

As you sit in the silence, notice the place where you feel the greatest discomfort or the deepest need. Become aware of your places of pain or your hardest questions. Let them come fully into your awareness without blocking the uncomfortable feeling of saying what they are and feeling what you feel. Dare to tell the truth to yourself about what is wrong.

Move from the confrontation with your own discomfort and pain to the awareness that God has come for you. The Healer is with you.

Are you willing to admit that you have wandered away from Home when you have? If not, why not? What do you get out of staying in denial about your shadow?

Psalm 107:23–32

Have you ever begun a great adventure, only to run into rough waters shortly after you started the process?

When did you start out on an endeavor, convinced that God was in it, calling you to it and insisting that you follow him? Did you ever start a great work for God, only to get out on the razor's edge of risk and danger and wonder what in the world you were thinking?

Teresa of Avila, the writer and great reformer of the church, shook her fist toward the heavens when things were unbearably difficult and shouted, "If this is the way you treat your friends, no wonder you have so few of them!"

Remember times when you have been battered by storms. Recall the ways God has come to you to calm the storm. Recall Jesus' words to the storm, "Peace, be still!"

Today, as you are in silence, remember the One who calms storms. That is part of God's job description, and he does that job well, but on his own timetable and in his own way. Sometimes he quiets the storms; at other times he calms his child within in the storm. Sometimes he seems to allow a storm to rage we finally surrender.

As you think about a storm in your own life, breathe and pray, "Peace, be still." Hear it as if God is speaking it to you. Say it until you feel it. Say it until you know it. Pray it until it becomes part of you.

Sometimes the storm is the rush of emotion, flooding our consciousness and washing us out into the sea of uncertainty or fear. God can calm the storm of emotion.

Psalm 107:30-43

DAY SEVEN

Today, focus your attention on the God who provides. Rest in the presence of the One who has unlimited resources, who knows how to make things happen, and whose desire is to provide for his children.

If you must, glance now and then at your inadequacies and insufficiencies, but gaze in your mind's eye at the One who is adequate. Affirm that his sufficiency is your reference point and your controlling thought.

If you must, take an inventory of the places in your life where there isn't enough of something, but bring your mind back to the One who is enough. God has enough, and God is in the business of working amid what seems to be impossible circumstances.

The key to God's freedom to work is often our willingness to get out of the way. "Let go and let God," a slogan of recovering people around the globe, has deep and personal meaning and power. Do you dare to try its wisdom?

Breathe out your tendency to focus on limited and limiting beliefs, both the ones you know and the ones that are unavailable to your conscious mind.

Breathe in the adequacy of God. Repeat the gentle guidance, "Let go and let God." Take it with you throughout the day. Make it your own. Call it up when you feel you don't have what you need. Let God work.

Faith in God ebbs and flows. God is constant, but dynamic and alive. Work with him, not against him. Cooperate with God's activity and let God be God.

Who Am I to God?

Healing the Self-image

Following close behind the God-image in importance is the image we hold of ourselves. In some mysterious way, how we see God shapes how we see ourselves. How we feel about God somehow affects how we feel about ourselves. Made in the very image of God and reflecting that image, we need to know ourselves as the *imago dei*, the very image of God.

The God-image is formed in those earliest months of life, and so is the self-image. By taking the psalms into the deepest corners of your mind and heart during meditation, the truth about who you are will begin to permeate your consciousness. It is as if the Holy Spirit of God, the Divine Therapist, goes to work through the power of the psalmist's words, weeds out false images of self, and replaces them with God's idea of who you are.

Furthermore, as the ancient words are allowed to move more deeply into your heart in prayer, you will grow more and more aware of your true self, the essence of who you are. Increasingly, you will be less identified with the false self, the ego, your roles and personas. You will feel the connection to the true self, the kingdom of God that is within.

The writer of Proverbs wrote, "Guard your heart with all diligence, for out of it flow the issues of life" (4:23).

Meditating on God's point of view of who you are is a way to guard your heart, that center of consciousness where mind, will, and emotion meet.

Who do you think you are? Is that who God thinks you are?

Psalm 8:1-2

DAY ONE

Today, begin by putting first things first, as the psalmist did. Focus your attention and your affection on the magnificence of God.

Let your mind wander over the bigness of God. Ponder the mighty acts of God in creation. In the silence, let yourself remember standing before nature, such as an enormous mountain peak, the ocean, or a vast desert. Recall the feelings you had as you experienced the grandeur of God's creation.

Let your mind roam the big events of your life. Recall the great mercy and grace God has given you. Move back into those moments when life was big and you experienced the bigness of God in life. If you cannot recall one of those experiences, imagine how it might be for you if you could.

Let your mind wonder at the mystery of God. Join, in your imagination, the throngs of people—adults and children—who have turned to God throughout the centuries, acting out of an inner impulse to seek God and an inner knowledge that God wants to be known.

Acknowledge the sovereignty of God. Affirm the holiness of God. Let your mind and heart stretch as large as they are able to grasp how "wide and long and high and deep" is the love of God (Ephesians 3:18).

Knowing the magnificence of God enlarges your sense of your own self. Placing yourself in the presence of a "big enough God" will help you grow into the largeness of your own true self. Do you dare to step into the largeness of your own life?

What would you be if you were who God designed you to be?

Psalm 8:3-4

Imagine yourself sitting on a starlit hill with the shepherd, David. Picture the pastoral setting with its gently rolling hills, the clear, vast sky, and the soft sounds of the night. In your imagination, breathe in the clean country air. See yourself leaning back on the soft earth and looking at the heavens.

Behind this creation, there is a Creator. Within this creation, there is purpose and meaning. As you imagine the stars and the grandeur of creation, let your mind wander to your own life and to the relation of your own life to the cosmos and its Creator.

Take in the wonder of this reality: The One who created the stars and galaxies is mindful of you.

Let your mind wrap around this magnificent truth: The One who placed the stars in their places cares about you.

Hold this thought: The transcendent, holy God who is sovereign and majestic has drawn near to you, through the power of the Holy Spirit. God, who so loves all of the world, loves you and places high value on your life.

It is not a faraway, distant, uninvolved deity who wound the world up and set it spinning in space. Instead, the God of the Scriptures is a personal God who draws near to you and wants to have an intimate love relationship with you.

Could it be that even turning your attention to the relationship of people to God is evidence that God wants to connect with you in a meaningful way?

How you see God and how you see yourself are connected. Do you share God's perspective of who you are? Is your view of yourself big enough?

Psalm 8:5

Male and female … made in the image of God (Genesis 1:27). Male and female … created just a little lower than the heavenly beings.

Who are you?

Do you know who you are?

If all of your roles were taken away from you, who would you be?

If all of your outer trappings were taken from you, who would you be?

Who defines you? Who have you allowed to define you? Do those definitions conform with God's view of you, or are they too narrow and constricted, squeezing who you are intended to be into a mold too small for your soul?

As you sit in the silence today, separate yourself from all the definitions you have lived with to this point in your life. Dare to move into that empty space of questioning and of not knowing, that scary space when you put everything on the table and become willing to know something you have not known before or see something you have not had the courage to see.

Ask God, instead of your culture, "Who am I to you, God?"

Ask God, instead of your past, "Who am I?"

Ask God, instead of your enemies, "Who am I?"

Ask God, instead of the person who loves you most, "Who am I?"

Ask God, instead of the person who needs you most, "Who am I?"

Ask God, instead of the person who likes you the least, "Who am I?"

Ask God, instead of your favorite, most cherished role in the world, "Who am I?"

Psalm 8:5

When was the last time you felt known by another person? Or have you ever had that experience of sitting bare-hearted before another human being with your true self hanging out? Do you know what it is like with the fig leaves of mask and persona, role and defenses down, with your soul laid open? Have you experienced the freedom of letting someone see your fears and fantasies, your failures and feelings? Could you dare that kind of intimacy with another human being?

Perhaps openness with another strikes terror in you. You may live with the feeling that if someone knew you the way you really are, he or she would reject you. You may not even know yourself very well. Perhaps all you know of yourself is your ego, that part of you that you present to the world.

On this day, imagine that you are in the presence of God with your soul bare. That Holy presence sees all of who you are in all of your magnificence. And when that presence, the presence within you, looks at you, the presence sees you as the beloved, the creation of his own hands.

Imagine that every thought and every impulse is known. Feel whatever you feel about having every part of your inner being known by the One who is Holy. Every part of you exists within the range of the holy gaze of God, and that gaze is a gaze of grace and mercy, of compassion and tenderness, of hope and delight.

Now move your attention to those parts of yourself that keep you from living "just a little lower than the angels." Can you see all the parts of yourself as God sees them? "You are the God who sees me. I have now seen the One who sees me" (Genesis 16:13).

Psalm 8:5

As you move into today's time of silence, focus on the phrase "crowned with glory and honor." Mull it over in your mind.

To meditate on something is to chew it. Chew on those words, slowly and thoroughly, with the intention of letting them yield their nourishment to your soul.

The glory and honor of this psalm likely has absolutely nothing to do with the glory and honor that the world bestows. This is a blessing that cannot be earned or acquired. It cannot be bought or given by any human being or any human institution, no matter how lofty! This is what you were made for by God, the Creator of the cosmos!

This glory and honor are intrinsic to who you are. They are spiritual qualities, bestowed by God. They are qualities that give you infinite worth and value, and if you accept those qualities from the One who created you, letting them fill up that hole in your soul, you will not have to look outside yourself—to people, pastimes, places, or substances—to fill the God-shaped vacuum that only God can fill.

Today, make a conscious decision to affirm this gift of God's affirmation of your value. Do whatever you need to do to remember this, for it is your basic nature. Write the words on a card where you can see them. Repeat them to yourself. Focus on what it means to be crowned with glory and honor by God until that knowledge moves from your head into your heart. Let the words embrace every part of your life. Live in that embrace.

What old self-concepts need to go in order to make room for God's view of who you are?

Psalm 8:6-8

DAY SIX

We are co-creators with God! We are not created to dominate, but to have dominion over what is our portion of creation. God's esteem for us is so great that we are created to be guardians and custodians and stewards of God's creation, invested with responsibility and accountability for how we watch over that which belongs to God.

In the stillness of this time, assess the level of your willingness to assume responsibility for your own life. You have been given dominion over a portion of life, starting with your own gifts and abilities, the natural resources written into the design that is you. How are you doing?

You have been invested with the capacity to reflect God's image in communicating with God and with others. You reflect that image as you listen and speak, resolve conflicts, and negotiate with others. You have dominion over your powers of connecting with others through language, both verbal and nonverbal. How are you doing?

You have been given the capacity to love and be loved, thereby reflecting the nature of the One whose name is Love. Just because you love imperfectly doesn't mean you can't love. Just because you have been wounded doesn't mean that part of you can't be healed. How are you doing as custodian of God's love?

You have been given the awesome responsibility of choicemaking. The more conscious and aware you are, the more able you are to make good, healthy choices. How are you doing, reflecting the image of God in your choicemaking?

In the stillness, reflect on your own life. Ask God how you are doing. Live who you are.

Psalm 8

Begin today's meditation time by silently repeating the last verse of this psalm, slowly and deliberately. Attempt to have the mind of a child, filled with wonder at who you are and who God is.

Let your eyes fall over the verses of this psalm, and see which phrases or words "choose" you. Those that seem to have more impact are the ones intended just for you. Perhaps those words are a guide for this day or for the next season of your life.

Perhaps they are words of challenge or comfort, of confrontation or consolation. Whichever words stand out for you, let them be yours.

Imagine how your life might be different if you began to live more fully in the truth of who you are, as revealed in this psalm.

Call to mind your loved ones, one at a time. See each one in the same light of this psalm as you see yourself. Does your perception of that person change? How?

Call to mind the person with whom you are in conflict or with whom you have a broken relationship. Pray this psalm for that person, asking God to help you see that person as this psalm describes him/her. Pray that the person might see himself/herself more clearly as this psalm intends.

Bring your focus back to the last verse. End your meditation time with the affirmation of the loving presence of God in every part of creation. Rest in this knowledge. Take it with you throughout your day.

How does knowing yourself in the light of this psalm change the way you relate to others?

Psalm 139:1-12

For some, the idea of God's encompassing presence is terrifying or constraining. Created with this awesome/awful gift of free will, we humans want to go our own way until we get in trouble. Some of us carry a childhood image of God's watching over us, keeping us from doing what we want to do. For those of us with that image of ourselves and God, it may be time for a maturing of the God-image and the self-image.

As you move into the inner chamber of your own heart, imagine that you discover God's presence really is within you. The kingdom of God is within you, and the One who made you guides you from within. The One who encompasses you with love is within you. The reason there is no place you can go where God is not is that God dwells within you.

Jesus himself said it. You can look all around you for it. You can try to find it in earthly kingdom and rule. You can place your trust in external powers, but the only true Power that matters is the indwelling Spirit of God, guiding you from within.

The presence is as close as your breath.

The presence is as close as the vine is to the branches, pumping nutrients into your life.

The presence will never leave you or forsake you.

You and the Father are one, a reality made possible by the ways of the mysterious, hidden power of God, alive and at work in you. (John 17:11)

What difference would it make if you decided to live as one in whom God dwells? Do you dare to live as one who carries the presence of God?

Psalm 139:13

DAY TWO

In the holy space of this time, take a trip in your memory as far back as you can go. Recall the stories about your birth. Perhaps you know facts about your mother's pregnancy. You may even know about the moment of your conception.

Take a moment to brood over the wonder of that moment when part of your father and part of your mother united in the safe space of your mother's womb. Can you imagine the Spirit of God hovering over that moment, brooding over the new creation that would be you?

Whatever was going on the external world at that moment of creation, God was there.

Whatever issues or agendas those who conceived you faced, God was there. Whatever hang-ups or defects those two fallible human beings had, the Creator was present in that moment of your conception. Mystery and magnificence surrounded that moment when life said "Yes!" through you.

Whether it was a convenient time for you to be born or not, God was there. Whatever weaknesses, defects, or imperfections were in you, God was there.

Regardless of what has happened to you between that moment and today, God was there, working in and among the various factors of your external world to bring about good and to bring you to this place of accepting yourself as made by God.

If you had a glorious birth, give thanks! If you are wounded and have lived as an unwanted child in any way, allow the Spirit of God to heal you from the inside out.

Whatever was going on in the external world at the moment of your conception, angels danced . . . and God was there, encompassing you within the womb of Perfect Love.

Psalm 139:14

"I am fearfully and wonderfully made."

As you repeat this line from the psalm, breathe deeply and wonder at the mystery of your body, the temple of God's Spirit.

In this holy space, scan your body and wonder. Marvel at how your feet and legs get you around, taking you from place to place as you will. Be amazed at your arms and hands, giving thanks for all the tasks they accomplish for you. Be glad that you have arms with which to embrace your loved ones. Rejoice in the acts of love your hands can perform. Breathe deeply and remember that you are fearfully and wonderfully made.

Ponder the magnificence of your body's organs and the intricate, delicate balance as they work together, keeping you alive and productive and creative. As you breathe in and breathe out, remind yourself that even the air you breathe is a gift from God. Let your breathing remind you, as well, that you are filled with the Holy Spirit.

Focus your attention on your brain, which lies all over your body in nerves and cells. What a wonder it is to be able to think, to plan and create, to analyze and conceptualize, to reflect on your own precious life! Be amazed by the power of memory.

Imagine the beauties of nature that you are able to absorb through your senses. What have you seen today that reminds you of God? Recall savory tastes you love, aromas that please you, sounds that delight or soothe you. When has someone touched your skin with tenderness?

Do you know—deep down in your soul—that you are fearfully and wonderfully made?

Psalm 139:14

DAY FOUR

If you were born healthy and hearty to two healthy parents who loved you and protected you, it's not hard to believe that you are fearfully and wonderfully made. If your environment was such that you were able to grow and develop to be the person you were created to be, it's not hard to trust yourself or be yourself.

This is not, however, a perfect world. We are flawed and imperfect. We carry brokenness and woundedness and awfulness, sometimes in our hidden parts where nobody else can see. Sometimes our handicaps show for all the world to see. We are nature, and sometimes nature is cruel. We are fallible, and sometimes we can't get past the appearance of things to get to the "fearfully and wonderfully made" part. Sometimes, life wounds so deeply that it feels as if God dropped a stitch while he was knitting us together in our mother's wombs.

Today, gather all of the hard questions and hurt places of your life and bring those things into the quiet and holy space of prayer. Read this passage over and over and dare to ask God if the truth the psalmist declares applies to the imperfections in his creation. Be bold and bring the most difficult issues of your experience before the Mystery, and see what mysteries might unfold. Bring your most difficult questions to God as many times as you must. Stay with them and struggle with them until you wrest from them the blessings they hold.

And as you rest and wrestle, keep breathing. Breathe in God's love. Breathe out anything that would keep you from knowing the peace of God.

It's easy to believe when all is well. Do you dare to believe when all is not well?

Psalm 139:13-16

As you move into the silence today, read today's passage several times. If you need to, argue with it. Write down your questions.

For this time, however, put the arguments aside. Decide to trust just enough to dare to believe that you are a person with meaning and purpose. Your life is intentional, guided and governed by the One who designed you. Beyond any external evidence to the contrary, there is intention for your own life.

Imagine that you are standing before the Designer and that it is possible for you to know the plan for your life. Imagine that God intends for you to be exactly who you were created to be, which may or may not have anything to do with what the big people in your childhood thought you should be. Have you adapted so much to others' expectations that you have lost your sense of self?

Imagine that the plan for you includes the radical idea that what you do in life flows naturally from who you really are. Imagine that what you are to do is to tap into your own unique set of gifts, abilities, and talents, and that your mission on this planet is to fulfill your own heart's desire and your own soul's code. Have you spent your life doing what other people expect you to do? Do you feel guilty and self-indulgent when you follow the path of your heart and do what makes your heart sing? Do you believe that it might be possible to make a living doing what you love to do?

Today, dare to ask God the big question: What do you want me to do with the days that are ordained for me? How can I get in alignment with your plan?

God knows the plan for you. You know, too. You may have to listen to know for sure.

Psalm 139:17-22

As you enter the silence today, reflect on the reality of God's presence with you in this time. Remind yourself that you are intended to live as a person with purpose and meaning. Your life is not an accident and you are not a mistake.

Gently, let the things that separate you from the presence of God come to your mind. Make a list, on paper or in your mind, of the forces that keep you from experiencing peace with God. List the things that prevent you from living the life you are intended to live. Include the afflictive emotions that keep you stuck, the lies you have lived with, the patterns that are self-destructive.

If there are situations, substances, or memories that you have asked repeatedly for God to remove, bring those to mind. Remember your frustration at doing the things you don't want to do and not doing the things you want to do!

Imagine God's presence with you in any way that helps you know you are in his presence. As you do this, bring to mind each of the afflictive behaviors, feelings, or thoughts as if you were bringing each one of them to God.

Perhaps some of these you can release into the hands of God. You may be so attached to some of them, however, that you cannot or will not let them go.

Is it possible that the things you cannot change about yourself are the very things that keep you dependent on God? Is it possible that the things you cannot fix are the wounds that turn your mind and heart to the Divine Therapist?

Bring to God what hurts you. Ask for his point of view. Let him help you.

Psalm 139:23-24

DAY SEVEN

On this day, get out of God's way! Make a choice to let God be the one who does your moral inventory. Let God bring to your mind that which needs to be healed or changed. Instead of letting your ego decide, let God work within you to do what God wants to do to bring you into alignment with his view of who you really are.

As you begin, read the verses for today's meditation. Read them slowly, one line at a time. Wait in the silence between each line and listen. Have the courage to hear the truth. If it is uncomfortable for you, listen even more closely!

Remember that in Hebrew thought, the heart was the center of a person's being, where mind, emotion, and will converged. Give God permission to untie knots in your heart, knots that keep you from living as a person with purpose and meaning.

Ask God to scan your mind and find the thoughts that keep you anxious and afraid. Ask God to go to work on fears or anxieties, afflictive emotions that will stunt your spiritual growth.

Be willing to let God show you behaviors offensive to him or to others, behaviors not fitting for a person who is fearfully and wonderfully made. Be brave enough to admit the things you do that do not fully reflect a person made in the image of God.

Admit the things you cannot change. Confess them. Ask God to work deeply, leading you in the ways that align with his intent and purpose for you.

Breathe out the old ways. Breathe in God's way. Trust him to know which is which! Trust God to do in you what you cannot do for yourself.

Psalm 1

As you begin working this psalm into your own inner landscape, read it over slowly several times, perhaps from several translations. Remember that a symbol points beyond itself to a deeper reality. In this psalm, the tree and water are powerful, universal symbols, images that can move your focus to deeper truths.

Let the words of the psalm form background music and turn your mind toward the image of the tree. Let yourself recall memories of trees in your life history.

Remember the story of the Hebrew people, wanderers in a foreign land. How appropriate for the psalmist to let the stability and permanence of a tree come to the forefront of his imagination as he pondered the ways of people in their relationship with God. Imagine the longing of the Hebrew people for a place to be, to stand, to rest.

Let your mind gather an inventory of the various places you've wandered, looking for stability and permanence. How have you tried to steady yourself? What have you used to anchor yourself in a world of uncertainty? What has worked for you? What has not worked? Let the visible tree lead you to the Invisible.

Let your mind rest on the image of the tree. In your imagination, see the root system, reaching down into the earth for nutrients and water. Let your eyes wander up the trunk of the tree. See the bark. Move your eyes to the upward reaching branches. Imagine lush foliage. Let the tree be an icon, a window opening to truth.

If you, like the tree, need nourishment, where will you get it? Are you "planted" in a place where you can remain stable, fed, and watered?

Where have you planted your soul? What nourishes your inner life?

Psalm 1

DAY TWO

Again today, read this psalm several times. Move your attention beyond the words to the image of the stream of water.

Picture the tree of this psalm, planted by a stream. Hear the sounds of the water. Imagine that you could dip your hand into the stream and refresh yourself with cool, clean water. Imagine the roots of the tree "drinking" the water and then pulling it up into the trunk, nourishing the branches and limbs, and moving out into the leaves of the tree.

Let your mind linger on the amazing way the water gives the tree exactly what it needs to thrive. Recall what happens when living things are deprived of water.

Let the symbol of the water lead you to an assessment of the state of your soul. Ask yourself how well you are "watered" internally. Have you planted yourself in a place where you can be watered, or have you managed to locate yourself in a place where there is no nourishment? Do you take time to drink the water of spiritual nourishment you need, or have you neglected this part of your life? If your inner life is parched or wilted, what do you need to do about it?

In the remaining time, imagine yourself as a tree, drawing up necessary nutrients through the life-giving water of the living stream.

Imagine that spending time in the silence is a way that God "waters" your soul. All you have to do is show up with the willingness to be nourished. The nourishing process, then, is up to God.

Jesus said, "I am the living water." How are you accessing that water?

Psalm 1

Who are you to God?

You are part of God's creation and God's responsibility. God wants to feed and nourish you. God wants to provide what you need so that you can produce what you are designed to produce. Meditation is one of the ways God has provided for that process of nourishment to happen. Meditation is a way to access the "living water" that enables you to be the person you are created to be and do what you were sent here to do. Meditation is the way you plant yourself in a position to be fed.

Through meditation, you "dwell" in the streams of living water. It is the way you are to live. It is the way of John 15.

And on what shall you meditate? What is the meditation that feeds the soul? It is the practice of the presence of Christ, a "chewing on" the ways and means of God, a dwelling in the reality of the loving-kindness of God throughout the day. This is the care of the soul that counts.

For today, dare to sit in the silence and simply love God and let God love you. Give up measuring the results of your quiet time! Forget about achieving and accomplishing during this time. Put your to-do list in an imaginary or actual paper bag and place it outside your prayer closet. It will be waiting for you.

Just be. Wait in the presence of God. Trust that God's nutrients are feeding you.

Are you thirsty? Come to the water! Are you dry and weary? Come to the water!

Be still and trust that the desire to be with God is enough. Let God do the rest.

Psalm 1:1

DAY FOUR

As you begin today's meditation, re-vision that image of yourself as a tree, rooted and stabilized by the source of life, the living stream of water. Your meditation time and practice is a signal to the Living God that you are showing up for nourishment to produce what you are meant to produce.

Meditation is your voluntary act of humility as you place yourself in stillness and silence before God, believing that this act of obedience is worth the time and the trouble, even when you can't see immediate results.

As you bring your attention to the first word of the psalm, "blessed," let your mind linger on the idea that God delights in you. The person who is rooted and grounded in the nourishment of God is described as fortunate and happy.

Being blessed isn't about entitlement or privilege. Instead, it is a description of a person who maintains the vital connection between himself/herself and God.

Being blessed is a mind-set, an orientation in life. It describes a decision, the way you approach your life with God and your meditation time. As a blessed person, you don't approach time with God as an obligation so much as an opportunity for God to reorient you around his intent and purpose for your life. Being blessed, you turn toward God as the roots of a tree seek water. You are eager and ready for what is good because you know God as good. Being blessed, you anticipate that staying connected with God through the act of meditation nourishes and nurtures you.

Being blessed is who and how you are intended to be. It is God's intent for you. How important is it for you to feel blessed by God? Do you feel that?

Psalm 1:1

"I have set before you today life and death, blessing and curse; therefore, choose life"

—*Deuteronomy 30:19*

"I have come that you might have life, and life in all of its fullness"
—*John 10:10*

Made in the image of God, you are created with the capacity to make choices. Breath by breath, choice by choice every day, you are choosing life or death, blessing or curse. Choosing life, the life of God within you, frees God to give you the fullness of life.

Today, sift and sort through your current choices and ask yourself, "Is this life-giving?" or "Does this destroy life?" Is what I am choosing blessing or curse?

Sift and sort through the people you have drawn into your life. Do these people support the life of God in you, or do their doubts, fears, and evil ways suck the life from your soul? Are the people in your life a blessing to you, or a curse?

On the other hand, do you encourage the life in others? Do your choices, your words and actions, promote goodness and truth? Or do you, by manipulation or power, intimidation or lies, suck the life from others? Are you blessing or curse to others?

Be daring enough to tell yourself the unvarnished truth. Sit in silence with the truth and remember that your natural way of being is *blessed.*

What do you need to do to live as you are designed to live, stable and steady as a tree, planted by the waters that will nourish your soul? If what you need to do seems too hard to do, ask for nourishment. If what you need to do is too costly, ask for the means to do it.

Psalm 1:3-4

On this day, revisit the symbol of the tree, planted by steams of water. Re-create the picture of that tree in living color with the clear, blue sky behind it. See the wind blowing gently through the leaves of the tree. Feel the breeze on your face. Touch the bark of the tree and put your hand into the water. Hear the song of a bird perched in the branches of the tree.

Again, let the visible (at least in your imagination) carry your mind to the Invisible. Imagine yourself as the tree, with roots deeply planted in the rich soil of the earth, fed by the water. Picture the foliage and the fruit of the tree, growing naturally and normally from the nutrients that flow from the water through the root system and into the tree. Wonder at the miracle of tree and water, sun and air working together to make the foliage and fruit that the tree was created to make!

Consider your own life. Within you is your soul's code, the pattern and plan for what you are to produce. Connected with the Source of life, the living water, you will naturally and normally produce what is in you to produce.

Your task is to place yourself in the environment where your gifts and abilities, your natural way of being and your unique vocation, can be acknowledged and encouraged, fed and nourished. A beginning place for that to happen is in the daily discipline of silence and meditation.

You can trust God to bring to completion in you and through you that which God intends. Meditation is a way of saying, "I trust you, and I'm available. Work through me. Do in me and for me and through me as You will."

Psalm 1:6

The rain, it falleth everywhere, on the just and unjust fellow;
But more, it seems on the just,
for the unjust have the just's umbrella!

Ah, life and its mysteries! How hard it is to see the fairness and justice in the world in which we live. How often it seems that God has turned his back on the righteous! As you reflect on today's Scripture, your mind may wonder to occasions and situations where it seems that God is not watching over the righteous, and that the wicked are flourishing instead of perishing.

In the silence of today, remember the tree. Recall the water. Remind yourself that you are blessed when you place yourself in relationship to God, and when you are blessed, you receive the nourishment you need to do what you were intended to do.

Remember that we humans don't get to see the whole picture. We don't understand the ultimate outcomes. We see, always, "through a glass darkly."

Amid the uncertainties and injustices of life, we keep planting ourselves by the streams of water and remember that "God's ways are not our ways" (Isaiah 55:8).

In the middle of disappointments and disasters, we return to the living water.

When life falls in on us and when we cannot see the hand of God, we affirm that the heart of God is good.

And we continue to know that while we cannot see the outcomes, we can know that God watches over us. There is no place we can go where God is not.

Return over and over to the truth that God is trustworthy. Believe it. Live it. Every day.

What Do I Do with Myself?

Making Peace with Being Human

Beware! The psalms do not give you permission to run away from the hard questions or the sticky emotions of life. While some of them offer a resting place from trouble and trauma, they are not a place to hide. They may give shelter, but they won't allow you to escape the unvarnished truth of raw human emotion.

In fact, it is in praying the psalms that you come face-to-face with the complexities of human emotion! There, in the middle of praise and thanksgiving, the full range of human emotions is allowed. In these ancient words, you can own up to your darkest nights and wrestle with your most difficult questions, all in the presence of God.

From the psalms, we learn that God can handle our rage and our terror. We can shake our fists at the heavens and cry out our outrage at the injustices of our lives. We can tremble and quake; we can moan and complain about *how life hurts!* God is up to helping us wrestle with our true feelings about our enemies, and sometimes we are shocked at the violence in the psalms. Any emotion known to humans is allowed in the psalms. Lying about them is not permitted.

Before God, we can dare to speak the truth. In the sanctity of the inner kingdom, we can bear to face the facts about a situation and admit, "It is what it is." Praying the psalms, we find the courage to beat the rules of a dysfunctional system that command, "Don't talk. Don't trust. Don't feel." With the psalms, we experience the healing of afflictive emotions. Praying the psalms, we are set free to talk, trust, and feel. Praying the psalms, we move into our feelings in order to be healed on the inside.

Psalm 56

Confronted by threat from the outside and consumed by fear on the inside, our common response is flight or fight. We are engineered to avoid danger or to defend ourselves, and we humans are infinitely gifted and resourceful in ineffective ways to deal with what scares us.

Today, take a look at yourself and decide how you typically handle fear. What are your patterns when something threatens you, either literally or psychologically? What is your treatment plan of choice when you are afraid? Do you hide in denial or do you lash out?

The psalmist was well-acquainted with the terrors of life, and Psalm 56 invites contemporary people to go into the pain of fear. It provides a way to take your fears directly to the Comforter.

For today, make a list of the things that scare you. Be as specific as you can in naming the objects of your fear. Admit the fear and own it as your own feeling. Give up blaming someone or something else. Accept it as yours. Notice your physical reaction as you write each one down. Remember to breathe deeply.

As you hold each fearsome thing in your consciousness, one at a time, reread the psalm. Move back and forth between your specific fears and the psalm.

Moving into the silence, offer your fear to God. Be willing to trust God enough to abandon that fear to God. Ask God to fill the void with love and peace.

"Greater is the one who is in you than the one who is in the world" *(1 John 4:4). Do you believe it?*

Psalm 56:1-2

As you move into the silence of today's meditation, move your focus from the things *out there* that scare you to those inner demons that keep you feeling afraid. Is there an inner saboteur that cripples you, ruining your plans and defeating your best intentions?

What about the inner critic that beats you up, torturing you with impossible standards and constant reminders about how you haven't measured up to someone's idea of perfection? How well-acquainted are you with the inner slanderer who won't let you enjoy your victories without warning you that soon, someone will find out that you are simply another fraud, trying to be somebody you aren't?

Do you have within you a tormentor who haunts and taunts you with threats about what will happen to you if you don't work harder or longer or better? Is there a tyrant within you that won't let up, shaming you and keeping you feeling defeated and downtrodden from within? Is there a persecutor inside your head that keeps you in a victim mode, no matter how well you are doing on the outside? Whose voice demands that you live in fear instead of love?

Today, move your focus to the omnipotence of God. Admit the existence of inner and outer saboteurs and slanderers. Live with a healthy respect for those demons, but dwell in the presence of the Almighty God, whose name is Love.

"For God did not give us a spirit of fear, but a spirit of power, of love and of self-discipline" (2 Timothy 1:7). *Do you dare to trust that?*

Psalm 56:3-4

Countless parents have taught small children the reassuring words, "When I am afraid, I will trust in you."

Grown-up children, as well, turn to this childlike prayer to ground themselves in dark nights of the soul.

Today, focus only on this prayer and let it calm and comfort you. If you are not fearful in this particular moment, pray it anyway, practicing for the times when you will be afraid.

Breathe out and imagine yourself surrendering the things that scare you. Be as specific as you can about the object of your fear. If you don't know for sure why you are afraid or if you are experiencing anxiety, simply exhale and say, "I abandon my fear."

Breathe in this prayer, imagining yourself breathing in the power and sound mind that come from God with the air that you breathe.

Breathe out and repeat, "When I am afraid . . . ."

Breathe in and repeat, "I will trust in you."

Dare to believe that this simple exercise of discipline can have a profound effect on your inner kingdom. Dare to trust in the economy of a simple, humble prayer. Take a risk and throw yourself at the mercy of God.

In the end, there are only two emotions—love and fear. Everything rises from one of those two motivations. Which will you choose?

We are advised to "fear not!" and to "love one another." Take the risk! Do it!

Psalm 56:5-6

DAY FOUR

It would be wonderful if we could take a stand against our afflictive emotions and our crippling fears once and for all and be done with them! The truth is that eternal vigilance over our own emotional life is the price of inner freedom. Serenity is bought with a price, and the price is paid day by day.

It would be a good thing if we could name our demons and tease out the shadow and cast them out of our lives forever. If only insight and awareness were enough! The truth is that the parts of ourselves that will work to overthrow us are always there. The moment I think that character defect is not there, lurking in the darkness and waiting for me to look the other way, I am doomed to be done in by the things I choose to deny in myself.

In the silence and stillness of today, admit the reality of those things within you that work to defeat you. Join the fellowship of people like Paul who know that "the things I want to do, I do not do, and the things I don't want to do, I do!" (Romans 7:18-20). Join the human race!

At the same time, you admit the things in yourself that you cannot change, affirm the power of God at work in your innermost being, healing the places you cannot get to by will or cunning. Ask for and accept the work of an omnipotent God who is able to undo the emotional programming of a lifetime and heal the afflictive emotions that trap you.

Every time you are tempted to succumb to the powers that would defeat you, return to the prayer of children of all ages: When I am afraid, I will trust in You.

Psalm 56:7-9

Now and then, we are pushed to the end of our resources. Occasionally, as we make our way through the tangled webs of life and its difficulties, we come face-to-face with the limits of our abilities and our glaring inadequacies to change the things that would defeat us.

The psalmist understood the outer reaches of despair and terror, and it was out of a personal, vital love relationship with the Creator that he was able to plead, *"Do something!"*

In the stillness, bring to consciousness the most troubling parts of your life. Feel the weight of them. Weep them. Lament them, just as the psalmist did. Tell God how much it hurts. Lay it all out; hold nothing back.

Hear the cry of your own heart to God, *"Do something!"*

As you wait in the silence, let yourself be willing to let God work things out by his design. Dare to become willing to give up your agenda and your attachment to one outcome or another. Trust God, who made you and knows you and loves you, to accomplish in you and for you and through you what he has in mind.

As you remain in the silence, keep breathing. Breathe out your terror and anguish. Give it up to the heart of the Almighty.

Breathe in the mercy, grace, and peace of Unconditional Love.

Breathe out your idea of how things should be.

Breathe in your confidence in the One who holds the whole world in his heart.

What is the one thing you can't yet release to God? Would you reconsider letting go?

Psalm 56:10-11

Make a commitment in today's silence to the affirmation in verses 10-11. For this period of time, dwell only on God as the ultimate Resource in the places that scare you. Focus your mind and heart on the presence of God, in whom there is no fear.

Breathe in the power and peace of God. Breathe out your fear.

Make another commitment to carrying the reality of this prayer into the ordinary moments of your life.

When you are confronted with bad news, reaffirm this prayer.

When you are attacked by another person or drawn into a conflict with another, breathe this prayer.

When you are asked to face a challenge for which you are not prepared, breathe this prayer. When you are tempted to return to a self-defeating thought, attitude, or behavior, breathe this prayer.

When it appears that your dreams are dashed against the walls of failure or defeat, breathe this prayer. When you have betrayed yourself or another person, or when you have been betrayed, breathe this prayer. When you can point to no particular stimulus, but you are suddenly overwhelmed by uneasiness, anxiety, fear, or terror, breathe this prayer.

Always, seek shelter in the presence of God. Let God's omnipotence be the measure of your expectation. Let the adequacy of God meet you at the point of your inadequacy.

Stand up to your fears! Be bold in the face of what scares you! Trust in God.

Psalm 56:12

DAY SEVEN

Life is a roller-coaster ride, and it's an uncertain ride at that! You're at the top of a hill one day, at the bottom the next. What seems secure drops away in an instant.

Today, move into the silence and assess the depth of your commitment to God. Take a look at the depth of your devotion to God. Do you want the provision and presents of God only in the tough times? Or do you live your whole life in the context of an intimate, ongoing relationship with him, one in which you feel the confidence to call on him to help you?

Ask yourself questions such as, "What can God expect from me?" and "If God rescues or delivers me from this current crisis, will I dismiss him until the next one?"

Be courageous and ask yourself if you know the source of your strength or if, once you are past the battle, you forget that *God* helped you and you start thinking that you did it all yourself.

In the stillness, remember the provision of God throughout your lifetime. Remember how fervently you begged him to deliver you. Recall the terror you experienced in the face of real and present danger. Remember the fear that assaulted you from within as you attempted to do battle with the forces on the outside.

Sit in the stillness and give thanks for the times God has delivered you from your fears. Give thanks for the ways in which God has helped you conquer your enemies and fight your own inner demons.

Today, renew your vow to God, however you choose. God loves you enough to let you decide the depth of intimacy with him. What will it be?

Psalm 137

Read this psalm and be shocked! We tremble, don't we, at the thought of praying a psalm that admits our desires for revenge?

As you enter the silence today, ask yourself what feelings you are not willing to bring before God. If you can bear it, recall the times when you have experienced rage or raw, ripping hate. Let your mind return to the moments of white-hot anger or simmering resentment. How hard is it for you to be truthful with yourself about these feelings, much less with God? How easy is it for you to admit your need to justify yourself to others?

If you cannot imagine yourself in the grips of such strong emotion, can you feel jealousy or envy? How often does irritation overcome you? Can you admit that irritation is repressed anger, leaking out? Can you admit your desire for revenge?

If you won't let yourself own your anger, is it possible that you ever resort to passive aggression? Do you "forget" things that are important to others? Do sarcasm and ridicule ever slip out of your mouth, stinging another with their bite?

Move deeper into the silence and feel the anguish of loss and grief. Remember what it is like when something or someone important has been taken from you.

If you have not yet experienced such emotions, let your mind wonder how it is for those who have. Without judgment, feel empathy for those who have tasted the bitterness of life. Imagine what it is like to bear the agony of hate and anger, natural and normal responses to the grief of loss.

How honest will you be with yourself? with God? What does it cost to lie about what you feel?

Psalm 137:1-3

As you experience the meditation of today, reaffirm the assurance of Psalm 23. Remember the Good Shepherd who is always with you. Hold in consciousness the affirmation "For you are with me," a reality that follows you through any valley of darkness or death.

In the stillness of today, let yourself be present to the losses of your life. Let yourself recall those things that were taken from you. Tell the truth about how you felt. And if you have not yet experienced a loss or are in denial about the pain of a loss, let yourself identify with those who have known the anguish of loss.

Your losses may be of people or places. You may have experienced the death of a dream or the ending of a relationship. You may have experienced the loss of health or the loss of sight or hearing. You may even need to grieve the loss of your image of yourself; maybe you have realized that you aren't who you thought you were!

In the process of grieving, we never feel like ourselves. We are, in the grief cycle, exiled from the way things used to be, and it is disorienting and disturbing. The agony of loss is compounded by the fear that things will never again be the same. It is natural to feel anger or rage at whomever we feel has caused our suffering.

If you are in a season of grief, let yourself feel the full impact of the grieving. Instead of medicating the grief, feel it. Instead of distracting yourself from the reality of what you have lost, go into it and feel it. Instead of lying about how much it hurts, admit it. You are less likely to act out your anger if you will own it.

The only way out of grief is through it. Let the Good Shepherd lead you through grief.

Psalm 137:4

DAY THREE

As you enter the silence today, recall a time when you were away from home. Remember a time when you were among strangers, trying to find a friendly face. Imagine what it is like to be thrust from the familiar and comfortable, away from that which has given you stability and security. Recall the sharpest homesickness you have ever felt.

That is the state of the psalmist, exiled and adrift.

Moving more deeply into the silence, remember a time when you felt exiled from God. Allow the feelings associated with the belief that God has abandoned you. What is it like, deep in the feeling of the absence of God?

We live, to one degree or another, in exile from God. We are, in a sense, strangers in a foreign land. All people know the foreign lands of fear, of hate and anger, guilt and shame, inadequacy and insecurity. All of us know the results of our rebellion, the anguish of knowing that we have walked ourselves out of relationship with God. At one time or another, most people experience the terrifying aloneness of separation from God. Often, repressed emotions separate us from God.

Make a decision to let the afflictive emotions be a reminder to return to God. Let that feeling of alienation and isolation call you back to your natural way of being, and that is in intimacy with God. Choose to see the moments of terror, when your song is stuck in your throat, as the touch of God upon your heart, urging you to draw near to his heart. Let your heartbreaks lead you to God.

And if you have not yet experienced alienation from God, pray for those who do.

"You will seek me and find me when you seek me with all your heart"
(Jeremiah 28:13).

Psalm 137:5-6

Sometimes, you have to stay in something until you get out of it what is in it, or else when you get out of it, you will go right back into it!

In the stillness of today, glance back over your life and recall the lessons you have had to learn over and over. Notice the ways you have resisted learning from the hard knocks of life. Has God had to use a two-by-four when a feather should have gotten your attention? Have you ever given up right before you got to the miracle or the solution?

When you are in an uncomfortable and distasteful state, it may be appropriate to figure out a way to get out of it. What about a state like the exiled children of Israel who had to endure the loneliness of the loss of place and home?

Bring to mind an unsatisfactory or painful part of your life. Tell yourself the truth about how it feels to be trapped in a prison of your own making. Be honest about your responsibility in getting you there. Brace yourself to endure the situation for a time.

Bring to your mind the reality of the presence of God, who promises never to leave you or forsake you. Let yourself imagine the presence of God drawing near to you in the depths of your heartache.

Realize that the activity of God within the person motivates the lament, directed toward God. God, at work in the depths of the agony, enables you to cry out for God. God, in the longing, makes you plead for God.

The One you seek seeks you. Do you believe that?

Psalm 137:7-9

DAY FIVE

As you enter into the silence and move into the depth of this psalm, you are face-to-face with horrific incidents and situations. You sit with those sufferings that seem to go on and on, creating unbearable heartache and difficulty for others. You make yourself look at the cruel realities of life, refusing to shrink back in horror. *God is with you in the most terrible places.*

As you bring to mind the horrors inflicted on human beings by others, realize that praying the psalms creates a holy space in which you can deal with the human tendency to want vengeance. Admit your desire for God to give mercy to you and justice to your enemies. Confess the terrible tendency to want God to protect you from the logical consequences of your behavior, while at the same time, you want him to punish others. Allow yourself to admit your self-serving prayers for revenge and vindication for yourself.

Remember the times when you have wanted to scream at God, "Why won't you do something about this?" and "Can't you see what is happening?" Admit to God, in prayer, the darkest impulses of your mind and heart.

Admitting the feelings is not the same as acting them out. Confessing them to God, who already knows the depths of your own heart, is not the same as doing something about the problem, something that you would regret.

As you bring the depth of your darkness to God in prayer, you give God room to move into the farthest reaches of your heart. As you bring your darkness into the light, the Light has a chance to work.

Letting the full truth come out before God is cleansing. Say it to God and then let go.

Psalm 137

"Oh, God! Do something!"
"Oh, God, I can't bear this another day!"
"Oh, God, why won't you intervene?"

The prayers of the people, offered in anguish and in mourning, do not fall on deaf ears.

Today, as you rest in the silence, don't seek answers. Simply wait in the silence.

Don't look here or there for God to act. Simply rest for now, and trust that God will act.

Don't rush ahead. Don't create pictures of bad outcomes. Give up worry, for just twenty minutes. If you can't do that, give it up for one breath at a time.

In the silence, breathe deeply. Repeat the counsel from the book of James: "Draw near to God and God will draw near to you" (James 4:8). Breathe the prayer, in and out.

Decide to allow the unseen power of God to move into your heart and help make you able to bear the unbearable. Give up your need to know how God will work. Wait for God.

Sitting with what you feel that you cannot bear, breathe ever more deeply, and let each breath signify a deeper surrender of yourself to God.

Surrender the problem to God. Give God time to work. Choose God's timetable.

Surrender yourself to God. Give God room to work. Choose God's outcomes.

Surrender your feelings to God. Give God permission to transform you.

In the silence, affirm that God has already drawn near to you. Accept that God is near.

Psalms 137 and 138

If you were God, how would you treat you?

If you were God, how would you treat your enemies?

If you were God, how would you mediate a conflict between two of your children, both of whom you love?

If you were God, what would you do when one of your children injures or destroys another?

Whose side is God on, anyway?

Today, as you enter the silence, reaffirm the sovereignty and mercy of God. As you remain in the silence, allow yourself to reflect on your need for revenge and God's need for mercy and grace. Ponder the reality of your desires for vindication of yourself and God's intent for redemption for all. Let your mind linger on your need to get even, to win, to have power over, to control; now reflect on God's agenda to heal, to empower, to liberate, to love. Remember that where love is lacking, power and control rush in.

In the silence, bring your unanswered questions and tormenting dilemmas to God. Surrender to God your need to control outcomes. Confess your inability to control your own emotions. Acknowledge your desire to play God in situations.

Resting deeper in the grace and mercy of the silence, allow yourself to remember that vengeance is God's purview, and not yours. Before it is too late, surrender your need for revenge. Give up your will to harm others, no matter how much you think they deserve it. Choose to walk in peace, to speak peace, to make peace—as hard as that is.

Resentment is like taking poison and waiting for the other person to die. Give it up.

Psalm 143:1-2

In the seventies, people plastered smiley faces on their clothes and declared, "Smile, God loves you, and I love you, too!" It was "in" to be happy for God.

Thankfully, Holy Scripture includes the laments, those bold-faced psalms of honesty in which human despair has a place in the prayer life of the human being who lives in the ebb and flow of experience and emotion.

For today, whatever your present emotional state, enter fully into the cry for mercy: "O Lord, hear my prayer." Feel with the psalmist that yearning for God to pay attention and to do something! Imagine an intimacy with the Creator so deep that nothing has to be hidden. Imagine a relationship with God so close that you know you can cry out to God with confidence. God will hear you.

As you wait in the silence of today's meditation, focus your attention on God's faithfulness and righteousness. Let your mind expand enough to wrap around the bigness of God's faithfulness, and when you think that you cannot stretch to imagine that faithfulness, stretch a little more. Accept that God is righteous and that God is at work in you and in your situation.

Around the world, followers of the twelve steps for recovery of a myriad of addictions take the first three steps over and over. They admit, "I can't. He can. And I'm going to let him." That is the spirit of this penitential psalm.

In the silence, live in the humility of letting go. Pray for the grace to let God work. Even the ability to pray "O Lord, hear my prayer" is evidence of God's mercy.

Through the day, when worry sets in, pray the first two verses of this psalm. Let go.

Psalm 143:3-4

This is the psalm for those times when your strength is gone and all you can do is wail your desperation. This is the psalm for those dark nights of the soul when it seems that all is lost, or when you are trapped and don't know where to turn. Pray this psalm when all you can do is weep.

It is often the roller coaster of emotions that keeps us feeling crazy and disoriented in crises. One minute, we feel strong and capable of handling the challenge, and the next minute, we are filled with anxiety and despair. We move from the biting pain to that lethargy of a "faint spirit."

Today, acknowledge the problem. Name the enemy. Call it what it is. Include the inner enemies as well. Name those afflictive emotions that sap your energy: fear, guilt, shame, hate, anger, inadequacy.

There is something healing in naming the problem. Lean into the pain of it long enough to feel the extent of it. Trust that you will not get lost in the pain, but that you will feel it enough to know what it is. Remember, always, that God is with you in the pain. He is with you in the truth as well.

Acknowledge that the Good Shepherd will lead you through the valley of suffering if you let him. He will not lead you there to leave you there, but you have to be willing to do what is necessary in the suffering.

In the silence, move back to the first two verses of this psalm. Know that the one who created you with the capacity to pray is praying to you. Open to his mercy.

God's Spirit within you leads from despair to hope and from death to life. Believe it.

Psalm 143:5

Today, begin your period of silence by remembering the gentle pastures of Psalm 23. Let your imagination lead you to a place of stillness, using all of your senses to create an inner landscape of beauty and tranquillity.

As you remain in the stillness, let your awareness move to what you are experiencing with your physical senses. Take a tour of each one and appreciate what you have heard, smelled, tasted, seen, and touched during the last few minutes. Allow God to be the Great Awakener, waking you up to the wonder of your physical self.

Become aware of what is going on in your mind. Be conscious to your thought processes. Are your thoughts life-giving, or do they sap your energies?

What are you doing? Are you resting in this moment? Are you still and focused or restless and scattered? What can you do to relax more deeply in the presence of God?

What are you feeling? What emotions have you recognized in this day? How are those feelings tied to your beliefs and thoughts? If you are flooded with pain and anguish, let that suffering awaken you to a deeper awareness of who you are and who God is for you and in you.

What do you want from this time with God? What motivates you to be still?

Remembering yourself and your body is a way of honoring yourself, the self loved by God. You are his handiwork; paying attention to that handiwork pleases God.

Recall the many ways that God has touched you and empowered you in the past. Recall God's acts of mercy and grace, the manifestations of God's love for you.

Psalm 143:6

Sitting in the stillness of this holy space, breathe deeply. Take time to arrive. Collect yourself, bringing your mind from what happened in the past and what will happen in the future to this present moment. Honor this time with God enough to be fully in this time and space.

Today, turn your palms up and rest them on the arms of your chair or in your lap.

Take the time to look at your open hands. See the wonder and mystery of their shape, unique only to you. Look closely at the lines. Ponder all of the tasks those hands accomplish for you; wonder at the vast knowledge you have gained through touch. Give thanks for the capacity to feel and soothe and nurture your loved ones with your hands. Remember the joy of holding hands with a child, a parent, a friend, or a lover.

Call to mind the times when you have clung tightly to people or things. Recall moments when fear or anger gripped your heart and made you clench your fists. When have you closed your hand to life or to another person?

As you look at your open hands, let them symbolize for you an openness toward God and toward life. Let your open hands remind you of the value of an open mind and an open heart.

Your open hands can be a prayer. They can make a statement to God about your willingness to be open to his activity and love. Let your open hands symbolize your consent to cooperate with God and your willingness to trust that while you cannot see his hand, you do trust his heart. Let your open hands represent surrender to God.

Through the day, when you are tempted to clench with fear, breathe and open your hands.

Psalm 143:7

"O God, come to my assistance. O LORD, make haste to help me"
—*Psalm 70:1*

Around the world, at specific times when serious seekers of God turn to God in prayer, the words of the psalmist remind us how urgent our need for God is all the time. Blessed indeed is the person who realizes the urgent need for God and is willing to live in the attitude of dependence on God.

There are times when our immediate need is urgent. There are moments when we feel so desperate that we plead with God to *hurry!* If you live long enough, you will know that intense moment when the need for God's direct intervention is so great that you think you cannot bear the moment without God's action. This psalm is for that moment. It is the prayer of a child who takes the parent's face in his hands and says, "Pay attention to me!" As you turn your mind and heart inward, where God dwells within you, hear the plea of your heart for God to *do something*. Recall the legions of other human beings who, in a moment of desperation, have cried out for deliverance and for mercy. Know that God hears the prayers of his children.

Know that God hears the prayer of the heart. Know that even the prayer of your heart is evidence of God's presence within you. As you breathe in, pray these lines from the psalm. As you breathe out, surrender to the One who is in all things.

Become willing to be still and know the presence of God. (Psalm 46:10)

Psalm 143:8-9

DAY SIX

Sometimes, we simply show up and open our minds and hearts to God. At other times, we come with specific requests. Notice, however, that in these verses the petitions are not for external favors but for spiritual gifts and internal qualities. What the psalmist wants most is what we need most, and that is evidence of the unfailing love of God. All of us need to know that God has not given up on us!

In the silence of today's meditation, remind God that you have put your trust in him. He doesn't need to know it nearly as much as you need to remember it. Telling God that you have put your trust in him will help you remember not to put it in worldly idols.

Hear yourself asking God for direct guidance, just as the psalmist did. Be willing to have a child's mind and heart and be shown what to do. During this time of silence, give up your attachment to your way and be willing to follow the guidance of God.

Hear yourself affirming that you open your soul *to God*. God may not need to know that you are choosing to remain steadfast with him, but you may need to hear yourself say it.

Hear yourself asking God to rescue you. If you need to do so, name your enemies. Be sure you know that the most dangerous enemies are those within your own heart and mind. Hear yourself stating that your hiding place is in the shelter of God's presence.

In the most desperate situations, it is sometimes impossible to articulate a prayer. Sometimes, all you need to do is breathe and let God interpret the plea. (Romans 8:26)

Psalm 143:10-11

Is it too much to remind God that others are watching what happens in your life?

Do we dare to think that God's reputation is on the line?

In what circumstances can we risk telling God what to do with our enemies? Do we ever get to name the terms? Do we have any clout with God? Have we earned enough points with God to get favors in return?

In the silence of today, admit the fact that sometimes you hurt enough to ask God *anything*. Bring to mind your wishes and fantasies. Tell God everything about the depth of your need for help. Give him all the instructions you want to give him.

Know that God understands our desperation in situations that feel life-threatening. We don't have to have our theology right or our doctrine straight to come before God and plead for mercy! God hears through our laments the desperation of our hearts, and he draws near as Comforter in the anguish of the moment.

In the final line of this psalm, however, is the affirmation of humility. After all, in the end God is God, and each of us is the servant of God. In the end all of us bow to the sovereignty of God. We can ask anything of God that we want to ask, and we *need* to lay out our yearnings and longings and needs with honesty and forthrightness.

In the silence, go to the Garden of Gethsemane. As you imagine Jesus in that dark hour, hear his words: "Let this cup pass from me." Hear the words of surrender to the inevitability of what is coming: "Not my will, but yours."

Even Jesus went through the agony of letting go. He is with you as you let go.

What About My Stubborn Will?

Creating human beings in his own image, God blessed and burdened us with the awesome/awful power of *choice*. In order that we might have what is good, he gave us the power to choose evil. In order that we might have love, he gave us the power to choose fear and hate, apathy and inertia. In order that we might have life in all of its abundance, he gave us the freedom to choose limitation.

Thus, we wrestle with God and we wrestle with our own willfulness, and sometimes we have to face our free will run riot. However, in wrestling with God, we often transcend our tendency to let others take responsibility for our choices, our mistakes, and our problems. In wrestling with God, we overcome our infantile ways and grow to the full maturity God intends for each of us. By staying with our struggles instead of running away from them, and by going into the pain of our lives instead of medicating ourselves, we finally find the pearl that is in the pain.

As we wrestle with God, we join the ranks of Jacob who would not let go until he wrested the blessing from the hand of God. We are the kin of Job who stayed in the anguish of God's seeming absence until the presence returned in a way that transformed and restored him. We struggle with God in our own Gethsemanes until we surrender what used to be; we go through our own Good Fridays to get to Resurrection morning.

If we can take comfort from the psalms, it seems clear that God draws near to us as we stand up to the struggle, choosing life, love, and liberty in him.

Psalm 55:1-3

Have you ever been up against something you cannot change? What's it like when you've done the same wrong thing over and over again, beating your head against the same brick wall? Do you remind yourself that insanity is doing the same things over and over again, hoping for a different result? Do you understand Paul's anguish over doing the things he does not want to do, and not being able to do the things he wants to do?

Whatever battle we fight on the outside, another battle rages on the inside. In fact, often the very thing we refuse to face internally soon meets us on the outside. Ultimately, we human beings are brought to the place where the struggle is between our own stubborn will and the majestic sovereignty of God.

On this day, name your battle. Call it what it really is, and then choose to do the inside job, the work of surrender and acceptance. Choose to call out the name of God. Bring him into the thick of the battle with you; that is, after all, where God seems to work best. His *adequacy* moves into place when we frail humans come kicking and screaming to the point of acknowledging our *inadequacy*.

Make a list of the ways you have tried to avoid confronting your own willfulness. Be ruthless in reviewing and accessing your history. Tell yourself the unvarnished truth about how you have tried to run your own life and, perhaps, the lives of others. See your issues of control for what they are.

Always remember that the only reason to put your life under such scrutiny is to bring your inner life into alignment with the intent of God, who loves you.

God created you with this stubborn will, and he loves you. Do you believe that?

Psalm 55:4-8

If this is a day when you are at peace with the world, give thanks! If all is well today, be joyful! If you and God are working together in harmony, savor that experience and be glad. And don't forget to pray for those who are struggling and wrestling with life and with God.

On the other hand, if this is your time in the wrestling match, take time to address your feelings about the struggle. Instead of fighting or resisting, let go and feel what you feel. Instead of distracting or numbing yourself to avoid reality, feel it all.

Name your fears. Name the terrors. Call them by their real names, and if you fear getting so specific, admit that fear as well.

Acknowledge the human desire to run away. Tell God how unfair you think life is right now. Remind him of how you don't deserve this situation, or admit to him that you have earned your way to this moment. Whatever you do, come clean before God.

When you can, say, "I surrender _____ to you." Surrender the situation to God. Surrender your feelings to God. Surrender yourself to God. Imagine yourself giving the situation into the care of God, who loves you.

If you cannot yet release part of the situation, admit your unwillingness to surrender that part to God. Admit that you think you can do better with it than God can. Acknowledge your fear that this time, God will let you down.

If you are willing to surrender, tell God. Go as far as you can in letting go. Maybe tomorrow you can let go even more.

Psalm 55:9-11

The God to whom you pray is the One "before whom all things are known."

Scary, isn't it?

Or, on the other hand, that reality can be liberating and healing. Since there is no place to hide, you might as well come clean and say what you need to say. Be who you really are before God. Experience the wonder of finding that safe place in your own inner kingdom where you and God meet with nothing between you.

Sometimes, what happens on the outside is so horrific that we know we can never accept it, and we want to tell God what to do and how to do it. We struggle with what is God's business and what is ours.

Sometimes we experience situations so evil and deceptive that we are filled with revulsion. Everything in us cries out "NO! NO!" to what we see, and that inner resistance is a constant torment, disturbing the peace of our inner lives.

Surrender is not a blind resignation. It is not giving up and giving in. Surrender is not a shrug of the shoulders and a hanging of the head in defeat.

True surrender is a clear-eyed acknowledgment of how bad something is and an intentional, conscious letting go of one's own will. It is backing off and giving God elbow room. It is letting go in order to let God work. It is letting God take care of a terrible situation.

Some situations are so difficult that we have to surrender anew every morning. Sometimes, letting go happens one moment at a time, breath by breath.

At the end of this psalm is the key to surrender: I trust in you. Can you say that?

Psalm 55:12-14

DAY FOUR

It's one thing to get into a power struggle with another person. It's another thing to wage an internal war, especially with the likes of *God.*

As you step into today's passage, remember the struggle of Jesus in the wilderness following his baptism. Recall the battle in the Garden of Gethsemane, and know that the living Christ is with you in your own battle with your will and God.

As you sit in the silence, you know that the battle of wills never ends. Each day, we receive the choice between self-will or surrender. Every morning, the mercies of God beckon the yielded heart, the heart yielded to the guidance of a loving God who longs to give you everything you need to do what you must do.

In the silence, imagine giving the control of your life to God. Ask yourself if your resistance has anything to do with your current understanding of God, and if it does, be willing to let your image of God expand.

In the silence, scan your inner kingdom and find the places where you still will not let go. See yourself offering those places—the situations, people, feelings, problems—to God.

As you inhale, imagine that the breath of God moves into your inner kingdom with healing, transforming love. Inhale fully as a symbol of your willingness to "take in" as much of God's love as you can hold.

As you exhale, imagine that you release your resistance. Exhale as deeply as you can, and then still more. Let that exhalation symbolize a deeper letting go.

God is big enough to handle whatever we think we must handle. Let go.

Psalm 55:15

DAY FIVE

Over and over, we are shocked at the vengeance throughout the psalms. Thoughts we dare not think, feelings we are ashamed to feel, and desires we would not want anyone to know lurk in the shadowy places of all of us, but when we read them in the Bible, they take our breath away!

Who among humans has not wanted God to punish those who hurt us and others? What human being hasn't had dark and terrible thoughts about another? What victim has not longed for retribution?

And yet, we fear owning our darkness. We fear bringing the darkness into the light because we fear the power of the darkness. We are afraid of what we might do if we know the extent of our anger.

The angry psalms guide us to work out our yearning for vengeance. Laying out the full range of fury before God—as terrible as it may seem—is a preventative measure. Telling God how angry you are in prayer helps you avoid unleashing anger on others. Prayer can be the safest of containers. It can provide the necessary boundaries in which to express the full truth and then leave it in the hands of God, to whom belongs vengeance.

On this day, imagine that God is sitting with you as loving presence. With God near you, dare to say what lies in the darkest corners of your heart and mind. Speak the words aloud so you can know what truly is within you. And then sit in the silence and truly hear what you have said.

Take full responsibility for your darkness. Then turn it over to God.

102

Psalm 55:16-21

In the end, all people will either disappoint you, leave you, or fail you. No human being ever created can fulfill all of your expectations or meet all of your needs. And this is a good thing.

Ultimately, all institutions and idols will fall short of giving you what you need. There is no magical other, no knight on a white horse, no quick fix or instant solution for the dark night of the soul. And this is a good thing.

Finally and eventually, all things outside of you will not be enough to fill the hole in your soul. And this is a good thing.

Surrender is not defeat, though the ego may feel that it is. Given the ego's inordinate need for security and stability, it is natural that the ego would experience any triumph of the soul as its own defeat. The ego needs to expand to allow God sufficient room to work in the innermost regions of the heart and soul.

In the silence, let all of the gods you have worshiped parade before your mind. Stop each of them and ask, "Are you really a big enough god for me? Can you really do what I need? Can you really give me serenity and peace?"

Today, imagine how your life might be with the God of all creation in charge of your daily affairs. Let your mind expand to contain the grandness of a day spent with God at the controls of your behavior, your reactions, your emotions, your thoughts, and your decisions. Let yourself feel God taking over, breath by breath.

If God were to take over the controls of your day today, what would be his first task?

Psalm 55:22-23

In the end, do you really have another place to go besides to God?

In the stillness of your meditation time, simply rest in God. Don't try to figure anything out and don't try to solve problems. *Just trust in God.*

If a troublesome thought bubbles up and disturbs your peace, let it come and let it go. Don't engage with it, for that would give it power. *Simply trust in God.*

If a worry or concern invades this time of meditation and prayer, give it to God and don't take it back. Like a little child who simply and wholly trusts the Father, cast your cares to him. Say the words, *"I trust in you!"*

If a feeling or memory annoys you and tries to interrupt your silence, put it on hold. You can go back to it later. For now, stay the course. *Practice trusting in God, one moment at a time.*

If you are tempted to fidget or fret, soothe yourself as you would a restless child. Calm yourself by breathing more and more deeply. Let go into the heart of God in a way that you can imagine. *Trust in God in this present moment.*

If, indeed, the power is in the present moment, be in this present moment fully. Bring all your awareness to this moment. Entrust the past to the merciful heart of God. Trust God with whatever is to come, and be in this moment at peace with God.

God must be accustomed to dealing with hard heads, stiff necks, and stubborn wills, for he made so many of them! Will you trust him with your own life and your own will?

Psalm 88:1

A woman approached me after I had taught about the long wait of Job. A patient at M. D. Anderson Cancer Center in Houston, Texas, she was part of an experimental program. Racked by cancer, but with an inexplicable light in her eyes, she said to me, "Only those who have not truly suffered question God. Suffering drives you to the place where there's nothing else *but* God."

This is the psalm of that woman, a woman backed into the darkest corner and forced to see that when you have nowhere else to go, God is in that "nowhere" place. Going there, however, is the scariest journey human beings face. The possibility that God will not be there is terrifying, but you cannot know that God is in that place unless you are willing to go there!

Today, recall the imperfect, problematic, and unfinished parts of your life. Think of the things you deal with over and over and over again. Face what you have tried so hard to change, the person you have worked so hard to fix, the struggle you think you have won. Feel, if you dare, the terror of complete surrender.

As you wait in the silence of this day, return again to the act of surrender. Regardless of how many times you have yielded your will to God, do it again. Regardless of how many times God has *not* solved your problem, surrender again.

When you have tried everything you know to try, where else can you go except to God? When you have given God every chance to fix your life, give him one more chance.

What will it cost to give God one more chance? What will happen if you don't?

Psalm 88:2

The Scriptures proclaim the faithfulness, justice, and steadfast love of God, and yet sometimes it is tempting to wonder if those attributes of God are meant for everyone else, but not for me. Driven to the outer limits of our ability to hang on and wait out the trial, we long to see evidence that God is at work in our lives.

This psalm is a stubborn psalm, a prayer for the hard-headed and determined. It is a prayer for times when you are driven to the limit of your patience and strength. Pray it when you have done everything you know to do and tried every solution you know to try, and the problem still won't budge. This psalm is meant for those occasions when the problem does, in fact, seem to get bigger.

Today, dare to move boldly into the presence of God. Remind God of how many times you have approached him and how, as imperfect as you may seem to him, you've trusted him to the best of your ability. Tell him you're back, *one more time.*

Let yourself hear the cry of your heart, pleading for God to intervene. If you can, cry aloud; give in to the frustration you feel. Feel the pain of your inability to see and hear and know the power of God. Tell him you're coming to him, *one more time.*

Confess that your own will is, at least for now, bigger in you than God. Acknowledge that you still hold on to some part of the problem. Ask God to do *in* you and *for* you and *through* you what you cannot yet do for yourself, and then wait in the silence, whether God speaks to you or not. Be quiet! Listen! Wait!

Ask God to reveal where you are still holding on. Then wait long enough to hear what God wants you to know. Are you willing to let go?

Psalm 88:3-5

DAY THREE

Letting go of my need to control an outcome feels awful. It's especially difficult to let go of something in which I've invested huge amounts of myself, my income, my time, or my love.

Letting go of my expectations, my fondest wishes, and my heart's desires is terrible. Letting go of my fantasies about how my life would be is like pulling strands of silk out of concrete.

Relinquishing control of my loved ones. Giving up a relationship. Letting the old die without feeling the compulsion to apply CPR. Allowing someone to be who she is instead of who I want her to be. Letting God be God . . . instead of who I have made God to be. It's tough stuff, isn't it, this surrender of your will?

Surrender feels like death, and it is. Surrender is the death of the ego, that organ of consciousness that gets you around in the world but has little to do with the soul.

We must, however, relinquish what has been in order to embrace what is. We must let go of what is not enough in order to receive the fullness of God. And it feels like death.

In the silence, ask God to walk with you into the agony of letting go. Even if you don't think God cares, ask him to be with you. Even if you are terrified—*especially* if you are terrified—invite God to help you do what you cannot do for yourself.

"Thy will be done" has to be the hardest prayer. Pray it at the risk of your ego.

Psalm 88:6-9

DAY FOUR

It's the abyss that scares us. When we think about letting go, we don't know if we will find safe footing or if we will gain our wings and fly. We fear that if we truly abandon ourselves to God, we will be abandoned.

In the silence of today, recall the times you have felt abandoned by others. Remind yourself not to project those experiences onto your experience with God.

Remember the times when others have let you down and the times you have let others down, whether intentionally or not. Those experiences were human, not of God.

Remember, too, the times when you were able to let go and let God work, and amazingly, mysteriously, synchronistically, God acted in ways that startled and helped you. Remind yourself humans tend to forget the manna of yesterday when confronted by the hunger pangs of today.

Ask God to draw near to you. Imagine that God does, in fact, draw near to you in this sacred time you have set apart. And never forget that *God* started this conversation with you in the first place. Prayer is God's idea, remember?

Breathe deeply. Let go and let God, and then *let go some more.*

You do not abandon yourself into a void. You abandon yourself into the very heart of God, who is faithful, steadfast, and full of mercy.

"I abandon myself into your hands. Do with me as you will." Can you pray these words?

Psalm 88:10-12

This is the psalm for times when you are driven to the darkest places. This is the psalm for times when all seems lost. When you cannot see where to place your foot to take the next step, when you do not know what to do, when you have no strength to do anything, *when you cannot go on,* this is your prayer.

This is the psalm for the moments of defeat and humiliation. This is the psalm for the times of intense arguing with God about what seems to be his terrible confusion about what should be done. This is the cry of anguish that echoes across the broken places of your life. This is the scream across the failed plans and the rubble and ruins of your dreams.

If you are in that place, go ahead and cry out. Scream and rage and rant at God. Hold nothing back.

If you are in that place, shake your fist at the heavens. Stand up to the God upon whom you have staked your life.

If you are broken and bruised and bleeding, wail it out. Weep all of the tears, and if you need to, weep some more. Great pain deserves great sorrow. Let your lament be heard. Believe it or not, the God of mercy hears you.

If you are not in that place, pray for those who are. Make sure you pray with as much humility as possible; avoid feeling prideful that you are not in that place. If you have been in that place and remember it, give thanks for getting through it.

A breath prayer for today might be simply, "Lord, hear my prayer."

Psalm 88:13-14

Surrender is no magic potion we sprinkle on our difficulties. It's not a negotiating tool with God. Surrender won't necessarily change the outward circumstances. It will, however, change you amid the circumstances.

Surrender is not a silver bullet, speeding resolution or slowing the ravages of a disease. Surrender won't make other people shape up to your specifications, and it won't make God be what God cannot be.

Your surrender to God does not change the nature, the will, or the intent of God. It does not affect God's sovereignty, and it may or may not affect the logical outcome of a situation. Radical surrender of all that you know of yourself to all that you know of God will, however, free space in your own inner kingdom for the love, power, and peace of God to have room to work.

For today, recall the attribute of God that the Hebrew people trusted through their wanderings and wonderings. Focus on the *hesed* of God, the steadfast compassion, unfailing goodness, and unconditional love of God toward his people.

Keep your attention focused on the *hesed* of God. Don't argue with the premise. Don't set up hurdles in your mind for God to leap, hurdles that sound like, "Yes, but . . ." and "If only . . . ." Simply rest in the presence of God, confident that no matter what happens on the outside, God's *hesed* is at work.

Name the most difficult area of your life. Imagine that you could hold that "thing" in your hands. See yourself holding it before the loving heart of God.

Psalm 88:15-18

In the stillness of today's meditation, recall the ways that you have tried to save yourself or others.

Turn your attention to the things you still do to try to repair the broken parts of your life. Ask yourself, "How is that working for me?"

Search your mind and heart and habits and see if you can find that one area of your life that you still try to control. What one area do you still hold back from God? What is the one thing you have surrendered to God over and over, only to think you hear him say, "I don't want it, either"?

Perhaps that area is your fig leaf, the thing you use to cover a shameful part of your life. It may your defense against disappointment or hurt. What you have not relinquished into the hands of God is what stands between you and peace, serenity, sobriety, or victory.

Ask yourself the following questions:

- What am I getting out of holding on to this one thing?
- What would it take for me to let go?
- What does it cost to let go? What penalty do I pay for holding on?
- What do I need in order to let go?
- Who might help me surrender this one thing? Who could hear my prayer? Who would stand with me and remind me that I have abandoned this to God?

Go ahead. Whatever you need to relinquish, do it! Then accept God's peace.

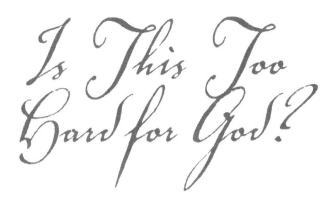

Is This Too Hard for God?

If you live long enough, you will eventually face the impossible situation, the unsolvable problem, the permanent difficulty, the devastating heartbreak.

Most of life is a process of dealing with daily difficulties and the occasional upheaval that requires a reordering of priorities for a period of time. When life explodes in such a way that we are plunged into deep trouble, we think there is no way out of the situation.

How do we live with the unthinkable horrors of life? How do we keep choosing life over death, blessing over curse, love over fear or apathy, and God over the darkness? How can we survive our devastating losses?

Praying the psalms connects contemporary seekers with a great cloud of witnesses, those who have seen the unspeakable horrors of humanity over the years. In praying the psalms, we connect with forefathers and foremothers of the faith who cried out to God in the most desperate circumstances.

We pray these psalms to confront our afflictive emotions—fear, guilt, shame, hate, anger, jealousy, resentment, and any other emotion that cripples our spirits and stands between us and the peace of God. We pray these psalms as we walk through the valley of the shadows of unbearable pain and darkest deeds. We pray these psalms for those and with those who suffer.

Praying the psalms, we pray from the prayer book of Jesus who stands in solidarity with the broken, the outcast, the marginalized, the weak. We pray these psalms as surrender of our deepest hurts to the One who is merciful.

Psalm 6:1

Pray this psalm when you feel that God is beating up on you, when you are driven to the extremity of your own endurance and strength. Pray this psalm when you are at the end of your rope and have nowhere else to go. Pray it when you are sick, either physically, emotionally, spiritually, or relationally. Psalm 6 is for hours full of loss and grief, when nothing you do gives relief. Pray it when you are sick and tired of being sick and tired.

In the silence of today, acknowledge the reality of God's sovereignty. Admit that what is happening to you feels like the punishment of God.

Using the gift of imagination, create a picture of the Great Physician moving into your experience. Employing your senses, make that picture as vivid as you can. See the Great Physician. Hear the tenderness of his voice. Feel the touch of his hand on the place where you carry your pain, regardless of what kind of pain it is. Breathe deeply and imagine the clean, clear smell of fresh air.

As you sense the presence of the Great Physician, imagine what that healer does as the two of you sit together.

Pour out your pain to the Great Physician. Tell him how much it hurts. See the compassion on his face. Let him know how helpless you feel in the face of such anguish.

Can you feel the presence of God with you, even in your agony?

"Lord, have mercy" is the prayer of the suffering. Can you pray it in this circumstance?

Psalm 6:2-3

Pray this psalm when the suffering lasts too long, when the loneliness is of cosmic proportions and the nights have been too dark.

Pray this psalm when your face the horrors of physical pain and illness. This prayer is not for the forgiveness of sin, but for presence amid intolerable suffering.

Today, pray this psalm for yourself, or pray it for a loved one. Perhaps you are in a state of health and can pray this psalm for those who have no one to pray for them.

Move into the recesses of your heart and hear these ancient longings, carried across the centuries by countless people brought to the end of their abilities. Hear the loneliness in prison cells and hospital rooms, the agony in war zones and nursing homes. Within your heart, stand in solidarity with the suffering of humankind, in prayer before the God of mercy.

As you pray, hear the cry of the faithful and the faithless who both plead for the mercy of God and know that even the ability to cry out is a sign of life. Even the slightest impulse toward the heart of God is enough to reach the heart of God.

Pray for God's mercy, goodness, and love to comfort the miserable. Ask God to draw near to those who suffer.

Moving within your interior life, bring to consciousness the parts of you that are sick and broken, dejected and defeated. Ask for mercy for those parts of you.

Psalm 6:4-5

Who do you think you are to implore the Almighty?!

What makes you think you can command God to do what you desire?

Do you really think you have the right to compel God to turn . . . to deliver . . . to save you? On the other hand, what good is prayer if you can't ask God to do for you what you cannot do for yourself?

In this silent time, imagine yourself being bold enough to ask God to get involved with what involves the two of you. Picture yourself asking God to intervene, not because you deserve it but because, after all, people are watching.

Envision a household of security in which a child feels perfect freedom to speak up about what he wants and needs. Remember the times when you have watched the utter transparency of a child who holds nothing back when she hurts or is afraid. Remind yourself that a child's survival depends on being able to cry when he hurts, and to expect the parent to hear him and respond to his need. This is the tone of Psalm 6.

Ask yourself if you are hurting enough to ask for help. Have you exhausted all of your resources, or do you still have one more thing you might try?

Are you familiar enough with the Almighty to get close enough to cry out for help?

What do you want God to do for you? What do you expect of God in your situation? Are you willing to ask God to act and let him decide how?

Psalm 6:6-7

DAY FOUR

What is your level of pain tolerance? Do you whimper and whine at the merest twitch, or do you wait until the pain is almost unbearable and the problem almost beyond solving to cry for help?

Psalm 6 is a prayer for the person who has done everything she knows to do. It's for the one who has researched every possible cure and stands at the end of the road. It's for times when money can't help because there aren't any more answers. It's for times when nothing can be done and the real foe is defeat.

The enemies and foes of the psalms stand as a metaphor for us, a symbol of what we cannot change. It can be an actual outside enemy or the enemy within.

This is the prayer of acceptance. We accept what we cannot change. It is not a prayer of resignation or defeat, but the stout, firm prayer of faith that says, "It is what it is, and I accept it."

In the silence, ask God to show you the places of denial and guide you into the light of reality. Ask God to draw near to you and stand with you as you face what you cannot change.

Ask God to help you call things—illness, dysfunction, situations, systems—by their real names. Ask for the spirit of truth to give you clarity. Become willing to know the truth, speak the truth, and feel the feelings you have about that truth.

Stand up to the challenge of trusting God. Dare to talk, feel, and trust—even in your pain.

Psalm 6:8a

On this day, move your attention from the outer world to the hopelessness within you. Let "all you who do evil" be the voices of hopelessness that torment you from within, regardless of whether your suffering is emotional, mental, physical, or relational. Whatever it is, your suffering is spiritual, for all of life is sacred. Nothing is beyond the scope of God's loving care.

Moving into the silence, let the voices of hopelessness speak within your mind and heart. Hear their taunting, but don't give them power. Let the voices have their say. Turn up the volume if you desire, but don't engage with the noisemakers.

No matter how weak or helpless you are because of physical limitations, you do not have to be hopeless. Even if you feel under attack from those who would make you their victim, and even if that is true in the outer world, you don't have to live as a victim. Hopelessness itself is a choice and a terrible illness of the soul.

Ask yourself when you decided to be hopeless. Is hopelessness a habit with you? Are you helpless or hopeless? Are you hopeless in all of life, or just in this situation? Is hopelessness taking you where you want to go? Is hopelessness a choice you can revisit?

Remember that hopelessness creates its own reward. It becomes a self-fulfilling prophecy. Like the psalmist, we, too, must take a stand against hopelessness.

Sometimes, we must say to the voices that taunt and torment us, "Away with you!" and "Be quiet." And we may have to say it more than once.

"Those who hope in the LORD will renew their strength . . ." (Isaiah 40:31). What is the object of your hope? What are you doing to keep hope alive?

Psalm 6:8b-9

DAY SIX

We do not fling our prayers and our cries for mercy into the darkness. We do not pray into a void. This psalm of anguish turns into an affirmation of confidence that God hears the prayer for mercy!

In the stillness and holiness of silence, imagine yourself in a relationship with the transcendent, sovereign Creator so intimate that you *know* God hears your prayers.

As you breathe, repeat the affirmations in these verses. Speak them softly, even tentatively if that is all the strength you have, and *know your prayers are good enough!*

If you can, speak these holy words with boldness and confidence. Speak them repeatedly until you believe them. Take them with you, and let them ride just below the level of consciousness, always ready to bubble up into a spoken prayer throughout your day.

If you choose, shout them with joy and thanksgiving. Speak them until you believe them, all the way to the depths of your heart.

If you don't believe them yet, you must say these words. You must say them over and over until you do believe them. In the material world, the rule is, "I'll believe (or speak) it when I see it." In the spiritual, Real world, the rule is, "I'll see it when I believe (or speak) it!"

Dare to say what is true! God does indeed hear our prayers.

What you think about, you bring about. What you speak becomes true. Speak truth.

Psalm 6:10

DAY SEVEN

We live, always, as earthbound spiritual beings.

We live, always, as people in process, and we live for the ultimate healing, the ultimate victory, the ultimate triumph of God over darkness and illness, difficulty and death. In the midst of it all, we deal with life "in the meantime," before the ultimate cures.

For today, use your imagination to see yourself as part of the large family of humankind. Be aware of the tugs and pulls of ordinary mortals and their choices on each other throughout human history. Feel the connection between yourself and all living things. Acknowledge that sometimes we must lean on each other's faith and borrow each other's strength to get through life.

In the silence, pray this psalm for those you know who suffer. Call them by name and insert their names in the appropriate places within this psalm. Affirm the mercy of God at work in all of creation.

Pray this psalm for those gripped with the illness of hopelessness, for those who feel trapped in addictions, and for those who are the victims of the choices of others. Pray for those who are too sick to pray for themselves.

Pray for the innocent victims of other people's violence and hatred. Pray for those who cannot ever be healthy or physically whole. Pray for their caregivers.

Pray for those who are oppressed by systems that use other people as objects. Pray for those who suffer in systems that defeat and destroy other humans. Pray for those whose suffering has been too long. Pray for mercy for all of humankind.

Where in this world might God be asking you to help him relieve human suffering?

120

Psalm 22:1

Read also Matthew 27:46 and Mark 15:34.

Today, let your imagination take you to that dark hour of the crucifixion. Calling on all you know about that event, imagine yourself standing at the foot of the cross, watching Jesus die. Feel the horror and confusion of that darkness. Hear his cry of anguish—"My God, my God, why have you forsaken me?"—and be astounded that the Son of God experienced the desperateness of alienation from God.

Dare to move, in your imagination, to the experience of Jesus. Feel the sense of personal failure of the human Jesus. Experience with him the humiliation and the crushing defeat of hanging on a criminal's cross, naked, exposed, and in physical agony. What was it like for the human Jesus to experience the darkness of alienation from his father? Did he, the human Jesus, know that there was something beyond this death? Did he question, still, on the cross?

Moving back into your own experience of the absence of God, remember that the Spirit of the Living Christ is with you in the darkest pit. The One upon whom Christianity is founded has promised his abiding presence with you, no matter where you are, and that includes the dark night of the soul. The One who promised, "I will never leave you nor forsake you," joins you in your own dying to self.

As you sit in the silence, picture Jesus with you. Use all of your senses to imagine his presence with you. Remember his abiding presence.

Even the ability to cry out, "My God, my God, why have you forsaken me?" is evidence that God has not forsaken you. Do you believe that? Do you count on it?

Psalm 22:1-2

As you pray this psalm, recall the times you have felt abandoned by other people. Remember the times you abandoned others. Feel the depth of feelings associated with those times.

Remember, as well, the times you felt God had deserted you, leaving you to make it on your own. While you remember, include those times when you went your own way, counting on your own capabilities, checking in with God when you needed him. Could you say that you have, on occasion, abandoned God?

Let the personal pronoun "my" rest in your awareness. Hear your own voice say "*my* God, *my* God" several times. What in you dares to address the Holy One with such familiarity? How can you assume this kind of intimacy with One whom you have abandoned and you feel has abandoned you?

Notice the strange and sweet irony in the beginning words to this psalm. On the one hand, you address God with the intimacy of familiarity. On the other hand, you demand an answer for his absence!

As you repeat the ancient words, "My God, my God, why have you abandoned me?" notice how close God seems. Isn't it odd how drawing near to God so often brings God near to you? How do you explain that?

Do you want God for what God will and can do for you, or do you want God for his presence? Do you want the protection and provision of God, or do you want God for God's sake? Do you want both the blessings of God and the burden of God?

As you go about your day's tasks, where is God? Do you stay connected with him?

Psalm 22:3-8

DAY THREE

What's with this psalmist, moving us from alienation to affirmation? He moves us from the pit of despair to the pinnacle of praise, and the roller coaster of emotion gives us whiplash of the soul!

Think through your days. Isn't life a mixture of the happy and sad, the up and down? Do you ever get rid of ambivalence, even concerning your relationship with God? Is there any moment of pure joy without a mixture of sadness hovering somewhere? Is there any gain without some sense of loss? Can you really sustain gladness without an accompanying sense of the pain of life? Isn't it true that life is neither black nor white, but gloriously plaid?

In the silence of today, bring to mind the blessing of the full range of human emotion. Wonder at the *possibility* of being able to affirm the presence of God in the midst of your deepest, darkest agony. Be amazed that even in the pit of terror or despair, you can still acknowledge the reality of God's provision in the past.

If this psalm seems alien to your own experience and you have not gone through the valley of despair, give thanks for that. Pray it, though, for those who suffer. Pray it for those who cannot believe in a God who draws near.

If you are in a season of equilibrium and equanimity, pray this psalm anyway. Let its words etch themselves deeply into your mind and heart, storing their power and wisdom for the future.

If you are in your own dark night of the soul, you must pray this psalm.

Remember times past when you called to God and he was there. He is here now.

Psalm 22:9-11

DAY FOUR

In the depths of despair, go back to the basics. When you've lost your way, remember the truths of Psalm 139. When you can't see the road ahead, consult with the Creator about your origins and reaffirm the purpose and mission of your life.

As you move into the silence of today, let your memory take you back to the earliest memories you carry. If you don't know the facts surrounding your birth or if you cannot remember your earliest childhood days, let your imagination create the picture of God's presence hovering over those earliest days of your precious life.

When you feel defeated and discouraged, go back to the original blessing of your life, a blessing that transcends all the human factors that were operative in your conception and birth. As bad as those might have been, God's purpose for your life is bigger and better. As good as they might have been, God's purpose is still bigger and better than anything human parents could give you.

When you feel that God has withdrawn from you, remember that God's presence has been with you from the beginning and has never left you. Reaffirm this truth, even if you don't feel its power. In spite of what other people have or have not done to you or for you, God's love has been constant. Today's task is to find that love and follow it through this valley of darkness and into the light.

Your feelings in the pit of despair are not the same as God's. Your feelings ebb and flow, but God's love remains steadfast and constant. Count on it.

What can you do to hold that sense of God's constant love for you throughout the day?

Psalm 22:12-18

Oh, the beasts, the beasts!

In the dark night of the soul, we feel that the beasts are all around, attacking and maiming us! Sometimes, daily life feels like a battle with the lions and dogs. Now and then, life gets so hard that we use all of our physical strength and are brought to exhaustion, depleted and devoured.

As you move into the awfulness of these verses, face the beasts within you. Regardless of what happens in the external world, the warfare within you is where the real victory can be won, if you dare to confront the real beasts.

Where are shame and guilt most likely to attack you? Don't those beasts know your most vulnerable places? Can you tell the difference between true guilt and false guilt? Are you willing to face the debilitating shame for who you are that saps your energy and makes you weak and sick?

Where do the beasts of anger and hate, resentment and bitterness lurk in your soul, waiting for the right time to grab you by the neck and slay you?

What about the beasts of inferiority and inadequacy, those demons that tell you you aren't good enough and you haven't done enough?

And how does fear assault you, roaring obscenities and lies at you and sucking the life out of your body? Where are you bruised and beaten by an overconcern with what other people think of you? Do you really want to die in the court of others' opinion?

Pray that God will be bigger in your mind's eye than any of the beasts you meet.

Psalm 22:19-24

If you can tolerate the darkness long enough, you will come to the point of knowing the breakthrough of the Light.

If you will wait in what feels like the absence of God, the presence of God will suddenly break through. It sometimes seems that God waits until we are almost to the breaking point to intervene.

In the silence, let these words linger in your mind. Dwell on the implausible and incredible boldness of the psalmist who moves from despair to confidence. How odd that those who wrestle with God come to the place of intimacy with God that frees them to ask for what they need from God.

Come quickly! Deliver me! Rescue me! Save me! These are the prayers from the pit, the petitions of the heart stretched to its limits! They are intended for the most desperate of times, and so we must not waste them on the small things.

As you pray this psalm, focus on the awareness that you live out your life, including your dark night of the soul, in the context of community. What you experience affects others. How you suffer your difficulties affects others. What you bring from the pit can bless or burden others.

You are a steward of your crisis of faith.

You are a steward of the blessing from the burden. You hold the pearl wrenched from the pain. What will you do with it?

In every pit of despair, there is a lesson just for you. What do you think it is?

Psalm 22:25-31

DAY SEVEN

On this day, if you are still in the darkness of God's absence, read these words with hope. With whatever amount of faith you have, affirm that this despair will end and that something lies on the other side of the abyss.

Affirm that your hope is not in your ability to hope. Your hope is not in a particular outcome or result. Acknowledge that the source and object of your hope is God alone and that in the pit, you stake your life on God. You gamble everything on God, who works in all things for the good, however God chooses to define good.

If you are moving out of the pit of despair, let God move you at God's pace. Yield to the recovery process. Surrender to God's timetable. Let God heal you in the way God wants to heal. Wait on God, who does all things well.

If you are already through the dark night of the soul, celebrate the deliverance of God. Give thanks to God. Give God credit for seeing you through to the other side. Some folks, after all, don't make it.

If you are through the valley of the shadows, do something to commemorate the process. Don't waste your suffering. Use it well. Let your wounds be medicine for someone else. Let the strength you gained in the valley give strength to another.

And if you have not ever experienced the absence of God, pray for those who do. Pray for those who have no one to pray for them.

As Christians, we understand that we are resurrection people. We affirm that there are many deaths throughout the life cycle, but we believe in life after every death.

Psalm 31:1

Where do you go when you have nowhere else to go?

What do you do when the doctor says, "There's nothing else we can do"?

What are your options when you're at the end of the road and you don't have the strength to do what comes next?

When you have researched as much as you can, when you have spent all your money, when you have attended all the seminars, read all the books, consulted with the best authorities, and there is nowhere else to go, where do you go?

When you are not good enough, smart enough, rich enough, cunning enough, pretty enough, strong enough, well-connected enough, *where do you go?* When you can't fake it or will it any longer, *where do you go?*

When you have come to the end of your own resources, this is the psalm for you. When you can finally say, "I am powerless over _____," then you know the refuge of this psalm. This psalm is itself a refuge. This psalm *is* strength.

If you are at that place of last resort, pray this psalm.

If you are not there yet, pray it anyway. The practice will be good for you. Pray this psalm of abandonment for the little things of life, starting with your own fears and your own stubborn will. Then when you get to the really big things, you'll have some spiritual muscle that will help you surrender the next layer.

If you can't imagine that you are powerless, pray this psalm for those who are. And then sit in the silence and hear the truth about your own powerlessness.

As you breathe, pray the first line of this psalm. Commit it to memory. You'll need it.

Psalm 31:2-4

DAY TWO

As you move into the silence of today, picture yourself in the safety of the presence of God. Make the mental picture as vivid as you can. Sharpen the colors. Feel yourself sitting in that place of protection and strength. Imagine God with you.

In times of distress, the greatest enemy is fear. In the silence, name those fears. Name all of them, even the ones of which you may be ashamed.

Breathe deeply, letting go of your deepest fears as you exhale. Breathe out the afflictive emotions that come between you and God. Exhale deeply and imagine that each breath carries more and more of the afflictive emotions out of your body.

Breathe deeply, as if you are breathing in the strength and power of God. Imagine that you inhale the guidance and direction of God. As you breathe more and more deeply, your mind clears and you are able to think more clearly.

As you sit in this sacred space, your rock of refuge, remind yourself that you are seeking shelter here for the sake of gathering your strength. This is the place where you go when you need to be nurtured and strengthened by God.

This sacred space is not an escape. It is not a bunker in which you hide for the sake of hiding. This is the place where you connect with God, tapping into the infinite resources of God so that you can face whatever you have to face.

What do you think God is trying to give you? Can you let yourself take it?

Psalm 31:5

Into your hands I commit my spirit.

These are sacred and powerful words. They are the words of countless pilgrims and saints who have come to the end of life or the end of their resources. They are the words of Jesus on the cross. This is the ultimate prayer of abandonment.

As you move into the sacred space of holy silence, sit reverently with these words. Let your mind travel across the centuries, from the cross to your present moment, connecting with the great cloud of witnesses who have experienced the power of abandonment to God.

Recall the other gods to whom you have given yourself—worry and fear . . . things and substances . . . people, processes, causes, and institutions—and ask yourself how well those gods have served you.

In this prayer, you abandon yourself into *the hands of God, hands that heal and help and hold your spirit.* Think on that.

In this prayer, you abandon yourself into the hands of the One who made the entire cosmos and your own precious life. Think on that.

In this prayer, you abandon yourself not into the hands of those who would use or abuse you, but to the One who loves you unconditionally.

Abandon yourself—your decisions and your will, your emotions, your habits and behaviors, your relationships, your day and this very minute, your past, your present, your future, and everything else that concerns you—into the mighty hands of God.

From now on, abandon yourself only to God. Do it every day. Do it breath by breath.

Psalm 31:6-8

DAY FOUR

Back to those idols, the demi-gods you've worshiped.

In the silence, name those idols. Know which ones you are particularly prone to worship. You can't avoid clinging to them if you don't know which ones are yours.

It's easy to name the bad gods like drugs, gambling, and pornography. We know the dangers of the gods of diversion, those good things that we take too far or misuse to help us become numb to live: pleasure, sports, shopping, hobbies, sex. They are out there, all in the open, with their destructive life-sucking jaws.

The more subtle gods sneak up through the cracks of your soul and get a foothold before you know it, demanding first place in your heart. Watch out for security and popularity. How about education and success? Marriage and family? Children?

Worse, what about the god of good deeds and altruism, fueled by the desire to look good and earn points? How about religion and church, the good cause, the holy war?

In the silence, acknowledge your own gods and then abandon them to the One True God.

In the silence, affirm, "I trust in God." Carry this affirmation with you throughout your day. Speak it anytime you feel yourself trusting in your own abilities or in one of your gods.

Remember that any other god will lead you back to a trap. All other gods will enslave you and oppress you. Only God really loves you and has the ability to lead you to the spacious places of freedom and abundance. Live in that space.

Speak it and pray it, declare it and announce it: I trust in God. And then live it.

Psalm 31:9-13

DAY FIVE

The recovering alcoholic knows he is only one drink away from falling back into his disease. The day the alcoholic gets up and forgets that he could slip, he is moving back into a dangerous place.

The person who has been through the dark night of the soul never takes the process of transformation lightly. Those who have come through that night will do almost anything to avoid going back into the darkness. Those who really know the process of salvation never take it for granted.

Someone who has been through the fire keeps a foot in both worlds, the world of God's deliverance and the ever-present reality of a regression. The real abandonment of one's self to God creates deep, pervasive humility and consciousness of one's humanity.

In the silence of today, assess where you are in your own process. If these verses describe where you are, admit the full extent of the connection between the physical and spiritual states. Illness in one area of a person often shows up in another area.

If these verses describe where you have been, give thanks that God has sustained you to a new level of wholeness.

Pray this portion of the psalm for those you know who live in this kind of distress. When you pray it for them, you also help yourself.

Pray this psalm for humanity. We who inhabit this planet are in distress, and we can join our prayers with the psalmist's prayer and ask for our collective restoration and healing.

Telling the truth about how things are and how you are opens the door for healing.

Psalm 31:14-18

In the silence of today, commit your "times" to the hands of God. The same hands that hold your will and your life can also hold the minutes and hours, the days and the weeks, the months and the years of your life.

As you rest in the silence, surrender your timetable to God. Admit your impatience or your indolence. Confess the ways you have run ahead of God or lagged behind him. Ask God to help you move with his timing, especially in the areas of your life where you most want to control the outcome and timing.

Ask God to deliver you from the enemy of procrastination and overscheduling. Ask him to help you discern only what is yours to do and to keep you from minding the business or the timing of other people. Confess the ways you interfere with God's timing.

Picture yourself sitting in the presence of God, warmed by his unconditional love for you. Imagine how it would be to have him "shine on you" with pride and delight. Feel the warmth of his approval of you, just as you are, all the way to the core of your being.

Don't try to solve problems. Don't carry on more dialogue with God. Don't try to figure out if your prayer is working. Just bask in the presence of God. Being with God gives you his perspective on the times of your life.

Imagine that being in the presence of God is the only thing you have to do today. Imagine that being in his presence is healing you.

For today, simply *waste time with God. Just be in God's presence.*

Being with God on a regular basis helps you know how to order your time. Dare to do it.

Psalm 31:19-24

When you've nowhere else to go but to the presence of God, you don't know for sure that abandonment to God will truly work.

When you face overwhelming difficulty, you don't know from the front end that abandonment is your only option.

Before you walk into the fire of the tests and trials of life, you don't know the strength of that connection you have with God. You cannot know what is in the heart of God until you dare to let go of everything else and leap into the abyss, and so it is that most people are dragged, kicking and screaming, to abandonment to God.

In the silence of today, return in your mind to the refuge and shelter of God. Recall the wonderful love God has shown you all the days of your life. Write in your own faith journal the evidence of God's love for you so that when you forget, you can read what you have written.

Stay with that love for as long as you can and simply love God. In whatever way you want to express your love to God, do it. Sing it. Write it. Dance it. Say it. Weep it. Or just be still and quiet, offering the silence of your heart as a love song to the God who delivers.

Call to mind the people in your life. See yourself as a channel of God's love to those people.

Finally, speak the last verse of this psalm. Let these words be the prayer that you carry with you throughout the day. These are your marching orders. This is the new way you are to be in the world. Be strong and have heart! Hope in the Lord.

The Power to See It Through

Some things never go away. Regardless of how much we work to run from that thorn in the flesh, whatever it is, it stays with us as a constant companion throughout our lives. *And that brings up the question, "So what do we do?"*

Issues like a childhood trauma, a character defect, a mistake or failure with far-reaching consequences, a chronic physical condition, or a problematic relationship can be the makings of spiritual giants or bitter, resentful spiritual pygmies, depending on how the person decides to live with the circumstances of life.

If the situation will not go away, it is possible to learn how to live *in* the situation in a different way. *And we are forced to ask, "And what is that way?"*

If this thing resides permanently in your life, it is possible to pull together the nurturing and sustaining resources that will ease your long wait between earth and heaven. It is possible to live with what you cannot change in such a way that your life is radically transformed by what could have turned you into a victim.

People who refuse to be victims support the decision to be victors. They form relationships with people committed to a path of recovery, sobriety, and serenity. They make their own personal soul journey a top priority, "seeking first the kingdom," and form stout, strong, consistent spiritual practices that create the foundation for an abundant life. Often, they pray the psalms for help.

Psalm 69:1–3

The power to work through difficulty is found by starting over every day. We must admit three things:

- I am powerless over this problem.
- I believe that God can help me.
- I am going to let him help me.

The pathway to serenity when facing a lifelong condition is simple, but it is not easy. We must start over, every day, as if we were beginners, admitting our need for God. The true spiritual masters know that admitting we are beginners is the starting point for wisdom. They also understand that if it were not for that problem that has driven them to the farthest edges of their own abilities, they would not know the empowering, liberating, grace-giving, merciful power of the Living God. They would not know the blessings of depending on God.

On this day, then, allow yourself to feel your need for God to its fullest measure. Stay in that place of neediness for as long as you can tolerate it. Acknowledge that you have tried many remedies and shortcuts, and that they, like your condition, have driven you back into the place of admitting your powerlessness. Acknowledge that you and God will have a relationship based on "one day at a time."

Even if you have no raging addiction or ongoing problem, your own self-will is surely enough to drive you to God. If it hasn't done so by now, it will, so go ahead and practice. Practice voicing your need for God.

Do you know the name of the "waters around your neck," or are you still in denial?

Psalm 69:4-5

How hard it is to know my responsibility in a situation! How tempting and easy it is to blame others for what really belongs to me. How hard it is to break the patterns of scapegoating others; how hard it is to keep from letting others lay their own fault on you, making you "the problem."

Today, ask God for the courage to stand naked before him. Ask God to expose where you are not taking responsibility for what you have done and for the things you have left undone. Ask him to show you precisely what you are doing to exacerbate the problems of your life, and then dare to write those things down.

The places where you have not taken full responsibility, the things you do to harm yourself and others, the issues you hide from yourself and others all act as a virus. Sometimes, those secret sins and personal demons cause a permanent failure in your life. *Isn't it better to come clean before God?*

In the silence of today, let God walk you through your moral inventory. Let God bring to your mind the things that are your responsibility. Let God guide you through a fearless, searching moral inventory, and then be willing to make confession and make amends where necessary. And while you're doing this, find a sponsor, a spiritual director, a confessor to guide you through it.

Isn't taking responsibility for your own life worth whatever you have to do to?

Psalm 69:6-7

DAY THREE

Today, name your "long wait," that thing you will live with for the rest of your life. Call it by its real name. Don't euphemize or overstate it. Say it like it is.

In the silence, imagine God is sitting with you as you tell yourself the truth about this thorn in the flesh. If you need to, complain to him that you are afflicted with it. Tell him how much freer you'd be without it. Tell him how unfair it is that you have this affliction. Rail against it; you'll feel better if you address your feelings about it.

Moving more deeply into the silence, still with the image of God's presence with you, become aware of the people affected by this thing that belongs to you. Name the people who are watching how you handle life's blows. If you can, imagine those people standing in a circle, with you in the middle.

Realize the full impact of your connectedness with everyone in that circle. Notice what feelings you have about how your choices or condition impact the life of each person.

We look at the crucifixion of Jesus through post-resurrection eyes. From the perspective of the human Jesus and his family, his life was a failure. Wonder at how that made him feel. How did his friends and family feel about his death on a criminal's cross?

In the silence, feel the mercy of God emanating from his heart directly to yours. It is a radical, life-altering, life-giving, limitless mercy, poured out for you in your situation. Can you accept God's mercy extended toward you? Can you give it?

Psalm 69:8-12

DAY FOUR

What's it like when your own family rejects you?

How does it feel to be misunderstood and to have your motivations questioned by your own kin? What do you do when a family member says, "We don't want you"?

In the silence of today, feel the effects of alienation from family or loved ones, the alienation brought on by the misunderstandings about this thing you carry, your thorn in the flesh. Feel the pain of family fractures; do an inventory to see if there is anything you can do to heal the estrangement often brought on by the stress of a family trying to handle a loved one's long-term problem.

It may be that your life with God is what has brought about the breach in your family. If so, is this because you place yourself in a position higher than your family, or is it because the family system will not stretch to accommodate a new thing that God might be doing through you?

On the other hand, if you are the one on the inside, and your family member is the one on the outside, is there anything God is asking you to do to heal that breach? In your mind's eye, can you see God putting his arms around all the members of your family?

If you have not ever experienced the anguish of family estrangement, pray for those who have. Pray for healing.

Pray for those who are outside the family of God, for whatever reason.

Pray for those who are alone, isolated, alienated, and afraid in our culture.

What part of you can you not accept? What is your disowned self? Pray for yourself.

Psalm 69:13-18

Partnering with God. Composing your life. Co-creating a master-piece with the Master Designer.

Does that sound grandiose? Other-worldly? What are your choices when you are living with that thing that will never go away?

Would you prefer to grind it out, living out your life in that gray living death of quiet desperation? How about numbing life, so you won't have to feel the pain of being human? Or do you choose to carry with dignity and grace the thing you cannot change? It is, to a large degree, up to you.

In the silence of this sacred time and space, imagine that you are in a space of peace and equanimity. You have come to the acceptance of the thing you cannot change, and now your energy is free to be used in creative, life-affirming ways.

Imagine that you have let go of the struggle, for this moment, and are able to wait patiently as God moves when and how and if God chooses to move. You are clear about what is God's business, and what is yours. The outcome is anyone's guess.

This isn't the waiting of passivity, indifference, and apathy. You aren't asleep at the wheel of your life. You aren't waiting for someone out there to rescue you and do for you what you must do for yourself. You are an active partner in this process, as painful or as difficult as it is.

This detachment is a holy detachment, and it is a supreme act of trust. It is filled with peace and, even, joy. This detachment activates deep discernment.

What keeps you from practicing holy detachment? Are you willing to partner with God?

Psalm 69:19-29

External enemies are hard enough to deal with at any time of life. The internal enemies, however, are the real problem, for you can't escape what's in your mind. These enemies keep you awake so that you are weakened and debilitated for the next day's challenge. They spring up, unbidden, at the most inappropriate times, spoiling your day or ruining your efforts.

The psalms make it clear that it is O.K. to ask God to curse our enemies and to get them out of our lives. They do not, however, assure us that God will do what we ask.

Imagine that your enemy will be with you permanently. It isn't going away, and it is going to give you trouble. *Are you going to let it ruin your life?* Or can you learn to dance with that negative energy in such a way that it doesn't always lead? What can you say to that enemy to silence it?

Today, let everything you need to say come out unedited. Lay it all before God. Then notice that, unless you have been struck with selective amnesia, that enemy still exists. Hopefully, brought into the light of consciousness and faced with strength, that enemy can lose some of its power.

If you have to do the same thing again tomorrow, do it! And again the next day and the next. Practice detachment as many times as you must in order to live with the enemy you cannot change. And let God do the rest.

What is the name of the enemy that seems uniquely designed to destroy your peace?

Psalm 69:30-36

One day at a time.
First things first.
Let go and let God.

All through your life, but especially if you live in the midst of a long wait, you learn to balance the opposite tasks of making things happen and letting things be. A dozen times a day, you may be swept from the despair of your situation into the praise of God, from worry and despair to worship and thanksgiving.

Know this: *The Lord hears the needy and does not despise his captive people.*

As you wait, then, remind yourself that God hears your heart's cry. Count on it.

As you wait, remember that you are not alone. Count on it.

As you wait, trust your way through one moment and then the next. Walk with the light that you have, even if there's only enough to take the next step.

Trusting, you obey with the best discernment available at the moment. You do the next thing indicated, even if that next thing is washing your hair or taking out the trash.

Face forward. Trust and obey. Wait and hope.

In the silence, you live in the present moment with the one whose name is "I AM."

Then, go to the next moment. God is still there, the I AM that you need. GOD IS.

What is your daily practice of spiritual discipline? Is it enough for your life's challenges? If it isn't enough, what might you need to prop your soul on its leaning side?

Psalm 86:1

Keep coming back.
The program works . . . if you work the program.

It is ironic that individuals who enter a program for addiction recovery talk about how fortunate they are to be forced into a daily spiritual practice. They "get to" work their program of recovery, and thus they receive the blessing that comes from the *necessity* of a daily surrender. Sobriety and serenity are utterly dependent on attending to the care of one's soul. Happy is the person who learns that simple but profound spiritual truth.

Israel and God were in a *covenant* relationship that was deep and wide and holy relationship. Initiated by God, designed for the benefit and blessing of the children of Israel, and based upon the reciprocal love between Creator and creatures, the covenant was limited only by the daily obedience of the people.

In the stillness of your heart, hear yourself cry out to the One who has initiated a covenant relationship with you. Hear yourself acknowledge your need to God. He knows that, at first, your need drives you to him, until finally his love becomes so big in you that you are driven to him by your love for him.

You keep coming back because you are designed to return to the One who made you. Every time, God calls you and welcomes you back.

You keep coming back because there is a God-shaped vacuum in your soul, and nothing else can fill that space but God. Every time, God wants to fill the space with love.

Every day, admit it. You need God. Every day, keep going back to the Source.

Psalm 86:2-4

"You are my God."

God doesn't need to hear the affirmations of his attributes. He doesn't need us to tell him who he is. It is we who need to speak our affirmations of the Holy One. It is we who need to know to whom we pray.

This isn't some idol made in the image of your mother or father. It isn't an object you can control or manipulate. This is the Creator of the universe, the ground of your being, the Source of all that is. This is the One who permeates all of creation with his redeeming presence. Take as much time as you need to remember the object of your prayers.

In the silence, speak the affirmation of these verses: *"You are my God."* Speak them over and over, quietly, as a way of anchoring yourself in the presence of the Almighty.

In your covenant relationship with the One who draws near, you don't have to speak fancy phrases or use magnificent titles. You don't have to impress God with many words and you don't have to come to an ecstatic high. All you have to do is acknowledge the life-changing truth— *"You are my God."*

In the words of this simple phrase, you renounce your autonomy and affirm God's sovereignty. Here, you remind yourself that daily you give up the control of your life to the tender, loving care of God. In this prayer, you acknowledge your dependency and your need. It's a good way to begin the day.

Imagine yourself saying to one of your idols, "You are my god." Think about it.

Psalm 86:5-7

You are forgiving and good, O Lord,
abounding in love to all who call to you.

In the long waiting period of life, it is easy to forget who God really is.

In the nights that are too lonely and on the roads that are too long, it's easy to doubt that God is at work and that God's nature is one of forgiveness, goodness, and love. When God is silent for a long period of time, it is easy to lose hope that he hears and that he will answer. Today's verses remind us of what we need to remember in order to keep hope—hope in God—alive.

Today, assess your feelings. Ask yourself how you feel about God and what he may or may not be doing. Repeat the verses for today and reaffirm his character.

Ponder your own intellectual doubts and fears. Go ahead and admit them, and then take your focus beyond your own questions and reaffirm God's true character.

If you are almost to the end of your rope, reaffirm God's character.

If you do not have the strength to take the next step, reaffirm God's character.

If you cannot even voice the words of this psalm, breathe and trust that God hears and accepts the prayer of your heart.

If you are currently in a season of joy, give thanks, and then pray for those who have lost their way. If you love someone who cannot remember the true character of God, don't tell her who God is. Love her in the name and character of God, and let your action be your prayer, lived out in a gentle touch, a patient ear, a good deed.

For one day, live as if you really believe that God is who the psalmist says he is.

Psalm 86:8-10

For you are great and do marvelous deeds;
you alone are God.

In the long wait, there are some things you can do and some things you must do. Sometimes, you must do nothing. At other times, you have to work as if the solution or the resolution were up to you. Now and then, you get relief or help along the way, but in the end, the long wait belongs to you.

Sometimes, you are face-to-face with the hard reality that there is not enough you can do to solve an issue. You could work hard for the rest of your life, and you still might not fix this problem. Sometimes, your best is not enough.

Now and then, when you face the limits of your own abilities, it's common to feel despair. Failure hurts, but it doesn't have to be fatal—unless you choose to let it be.

On this day, sit in the silence and remember the mighty acts of God in your life. Recall the small gifts of grace as well. Reaffirm that God is a God of infinite resources and ultimate creativity, and it is to that God that you surrender your life and all of your concerns. Repeat the words of today's meditation until you know them in your heart.

As you wait, remind yourself that God is at work.

Remember that you don't have to know all of the ways of God in order to trust God.

Remember that your job is to keep turning your attention away from the problem and back to God. Trust that God is at work. Leave the results up to him.

What is the area of life you most want to control? What could God do with that area?

Psalm 86:11-13

DAY FIVE

Ah, the heart. It's not a construction-paper cutout or a red drawing on a Valentine card.

In Hebrew thought, the heart was the mainspring of the personality, the place where thought, emotion, and will came together.

In today's silence, go within to that inner kingdom where the Living God dwells, and listen. Listen for the still, small voice of the One who keeps you safe.

Become aware of the various pulls on your heart, dividing its loyalties. Bring into consciousness the competing loyalties and the dueling duties that vie for your attention and affection. Admit your tendency to serve more than one master. Acknowledge your ambivalence about much of your life, *even God.*

When you must live through a long process of difficulty, it's easy to lose heart. It's tempting to switch directions and follow after another god, when it seems that God takes too long to show his mercy and grace.

It takes a great deal of courage to stay the course with God. It is no easy thing to keep on the path of single-minded devotion to God, especially when the gods of easy answers seduce you away from the hard path.

In recovery processes, the abiding truth is that "the hard way is the easy way." The most life-giving truths are simple, but they aren't easy. To keep your heart and mind focused on God and to keep on keeping on, trusting in God's way is a daily decision.

Who helps you stay on the path of the undivided heart? Don't try to go alone.

Psalm 86:14-16

But you, O LORD, are a compassionate and gracious God,
slow to anger, abounding in love and faithfulness.

Waiting in any setting, indoors or out, you can choose where to place your focus. You can see the colors, or you can hear the sounds. You can notice the beauty, or you can dwell on the ugliness. It's your choice.

In your life situation, your big challenge, you can choose what you will see. You can gaze forever at the impossibility of it all. You can engage with the problems and the pain and you can see everything that is wrong.

On the other hand, you can choose to glance at the problems, acknowledging them and working to do what you have to do. In the midst of every difficulty, though, it is possible to train your eyes to see the compassionate and gracious God at work.

At the beginning of the day, make a decision to look for God in your circumstances. Listen, with that ear of the soul, for the heartbeat of God. Watch for his fingerprints in the coincidences that the untrained eye passes over.

At the end of the day, recollect your senses and your self and take time to recall the places where God broke through your awareness, climbing over your doubts and fears to reveal himself to you. The more you notice God, the more you get to see God at work.

God is everywhere at all times. You might as well get acquainted with his ways.

When was the last time you knocked yourself out doing something for someone you love? How did it feel when your work was noticed? How did it feel if it wasn't?

Psalm 86:16-17

You, O LORD, have helped me and comforted me.

Within intimate relationships, human beings don't have to inflate their language to ask for what they need. The trust in a close, personal relationship makes it possible to say what is necessary and to be clear and direct.

As you live in the stillness of this moment, know that from God's perspective, you are safe enough to speak clearly and directly to him about what you need. God wants you to trust him enough to speak the language of love and intimacy with him.

The psalmist was free enough with God to ask him to act within the requirements of his character. He was on intimate enough terms within the covenant relationship to say, "*Do* what you *are*; act as you have said that you are."

Can you pray these words of the psalmist as your own?

Do you speak them timidly, as if you aren't too sure about the status of your own relationship with God? Do you hesitate, not wanting to impose or presume upon the Holy One?

Or do you step up and speak boldly and confidently, knowing that even if you falter, God understands? Even if you are afraid, God hears you. Even if you have blundered in the past, God will still do what he did in the past.

Imagine that God is with you as you pray. Picture the look of delight on his face when he realizes that you know him well enough to ask him for what you need.

And when he acts with mercy, goodness, and comfort, write it down. Remember!

If God were to help you and comfort you in the way that you need, what way would that be?

Psalm 84:1-2

Seek first the kingdom of God . . .
> —*Matthew 6:33*

. . . the kingdom of God is within you.
> —*Luke 17:21*

For the long journey of life, the best place to dwell is in the heart of God. In order to have the power to see things through, the best plan is dwelling with God. You can't visit God's dwelling place now and then and expect to have what you need for the big challenges of life. You must choose daily to dwell with God in your own heart.

In the silence, turn your thoughts to that kingdom within, the prayer closet of your inner life. You can go to that place any time, wherever you are.

That place within you could not be seen by an MRI or CT scan. A surgeon could not find it, but it is there within you. It is the dwelling place of the Most High God whose name is Immanuel, God-with-us.

Finding that place requires faith. The longing for that inner kingdom, a longing often activated by external crisis or internal need, is the summons to go within and meet God there. Go there in spite of your doubts, and you will find the place you need to be.

Countless others have gone before you and found the loveliness of the dwelling place. A great cloud of witnesses oversees your efforts. Dare to discover that this dwelling place of God is where you came from and where you are going. Open the eyes of your heart and see that God is within you.

What stands in your way of meeting God in the sanctuary of your heart?

Psalm 84:2-4

Dwell in me and I will dwell in you.
                                        —John 15:4a

Wherever you are today, you can dwell with God. In fact, underneath all other yearnings is the yearning for that dwelling place. Life's problems contain within them an invitation to turn toward God. God wants to be at home in your consciousness.

As you enter into the silence of this day, imagine that you are in the presence of God. In whatever ways you choose to picture that presence, hold it in your consciousness for as long as you can. God wants you to be at home with him.

Create a sensory-rich experience in which you can be with God. Make the details vivid. In your imagination, you can return to this place at any time. The experience of being with God is portable. You do not have to go to a cathedral or a chapel to be with God. You do not need ritual or a prompter to take you there. There is no place you can go where God is not there. God is your home.

Ancient mystics affirmed, "I dwell in the heart of God, who dwells in my heart," and "I look at the God who looks at me." They knew that "the One whom I am seeking seeks me." Life with God is about living in the presence of God who lives in you.

However deep your yearning for God, God's yearning for you is infinitely greater.

However deep your pain, that is the depth of God's desire to draw near to you and comfort you. Your cry for the living God is a mere echo of his cry for you.

However pervasive your need is in the outer world of work or family, that is the extent of God's longing to help you.

What do you expect of God? What do you need from God? Where is God for you?

Psalm 84:5

Blessed are those who hunger and thirst after righteousness, for they shall be filled.

—Matthew 5:6

Pilgrimage. It's a big biblical theme.

Righteousness. It's about how things are supposed to be.

What is the pilgrimage of a life if it is not a pilgrimage to God, a yearning for things to be as they are supposed to be, a journey to the true self? What is the true self if it is not being at home with oneself? What is being at home with oneself if it is not being at home with God?

And can you really get there—that place of being at home with yourself and with God—without the intense hunger and thirst that is big enough to force you on a pilgrimage? Would you really leave safety and security of the way things have always been without some big *push*?

In the silence, open your mind and heart to the possibility that you have received an awesome invitation to step into the largeness of your own life.

Imagine, if you will, that all of the constraints and restraints you experience are intended to send you on a pilgrimage to find your true self, a self that can be found only in the dwelling place of God.

What if this difficulty that goes on and on has within it an exquisite blessing, the gift of your authenticity?

What is the scariest thing about your life? Could it be that God is there?

Psalm 84:6-7

DAY FOUR

The Valley of Baca reminds us that we must not romanticize the spiritual pilgrimage. The way home to the place where God is and to the place of one's true self is fraught with peril and danger. There are dry places on the way home.

In today's quiet space, call to mind the image you present to the world. How close is that image with who you know yourself to be, in the core of your being? The greater the distance between those two selves, the more discomfort you will feel. Walking through the Valley of Baca provides an opportunity to let go of the false self and claim the true self. Every difficulty can be interpreted as an opportunity to become who you really are. Every challenge you meet in the long journey of waiting provides an opportunity to go from "strength to strength."

Ask yourself, in the quietness where only you and God meet, if you are resisting the challenge of the Valley of Baca. Are you in denial about what is really going on?

In what ways do you numb yourself to keep from feeling the full impact of your Valley of Baca? How do you distract yourself from the real challenge? Could it be that by avoiding the refiner's fire, you are avoiding the opportunity to step into the largeness of your own unique and precious life?

Are you blaming others for your Valley? Are you lazing around in the neverland of "what could have been" or "if only"? If you are, would you be willing, for just this quiet time, to walk deeply into your doubt and despair, your skepticism and cynicism, and change your mind? Would you be willing to know that God is in the Valley of Baca?

What is the life lesson you are being taught? Are you a willing learner? If not, why not?

Psalm 84:8-9

The value of a long wait is that it gives the pilgrim lots of opportunities for introspection. In fact, one of the most valuable lessons in the long wait is the lesson of introspection, a skill not valued by contemporary culture.

In the silence, ask yourself some questions, and then wait to see what answers bubble up from deep within your heart. Pay attention to the first answer that springs to your mind, but also wait for the deeper answer. Both may be true, but one may be nearer to the truth than the other.

Do you really believe God hears your prayer?

Do you really think God is attentive to your need, or do you live with the belief that God has favorites, and you aren't one of them?

Do you believe God is responsive to you, or do you believe you have to work harder than everyone else to earn God's favor or even his listening ear?

What do you expect from God? Or do you believe God expects labor and love from you, and then, someday, he will meet you at the point of your need?

Are you willing for God to bestow the favor he chooses on you, or do you want to specify the favors?

What do you most need from God on this day?

In what ways are you blocking God's favor for your life?

If you are in a season of grace or a state of consolation, is there anyone for whom you could pray this prayer/psalm? Can you pray it for your enemies? For strangers?

Psalm 84:10-12

We do not want to be beginners . . . we will never be anything but beginning. . . . The desire to please you does, in fact, please you.
—*Thomas Merton*

Return, every day, to the dwelling place of God. Return when you are bored and tired and feel that nothing is "happening."

Trust the process.

Return every day, even if you feel that God has withdrawn his favor and abandoned you.

Trust the One who called you to the pilgrimage in the first place.

Return every day, whether you feel like returning or not. It is when you keep on keeping on that God seems to find a way to give you what you need.

Trust the One who knows just where your faults are.

As you return day after day, you show yourself that you are serious about the spiritual journey. Your faithful discipline in the meantime will come back to you in ways you cannot even imagine.

Believe the words of Jesus: the one who *keeps on* asking, seeking, and knocking will be given what is necessary for the pilgrimage.

And one day, out of the blue, God will answer in a way that surprises you and thrills you, comforts and sustains you. God will meet you in a way so wondrous, so God-like, so extraordinary that you will never be the same.

Keep on keeping on. Suit up and show up. God is with you.

Is the question "Can I trust God?" or "Can God trust me?" Think it over.

Psalm 131

In the days when you are battered and beaten by the dragons and lions of life in the world, retreat to this psalm and its imagery.

Draw apart, even if you are in the middle of your life's battle. Create, in your mind's eye, a picture of yourself at rest in the arms of a loving, embracing mother.

Picture that mother as the ultimate place of comfort and solace. Draw her, in your imagination, as the ultimate mother, the mother who is always available and attentive. See her and touch her; imagine yourself nestled in her arms. Imagine how it would be for her to stroke your hair and rock you.

Hear the mother's lullaby, crooned gently just for you. Imagine that you are so close to her that you can hear her steady, faithful heartbeat.

Feel the contentment of a loved child, fully satisfied and nourished. Feel the complete safety of the mother's arms. Know that you are the beloved child of this mother.

Hold this image in your mind's eye and let your breathing become deeper and more relaxed.

Take this image with you and return to it whenever you need to soothe and comfort yourself. Give up your concern with great matters and rest in God's loving arms.

When you are overwhelmed and overstimulated, even by the wonderful things of life, go to this tender, loving embrace of God. Rest for as long as you need to rest.

Can you stretch your image of God as much as the psalmist did? Can you let God be mother to the child in you? Can you still your soul in the arms of God?

Forgive and Forget: Setting Grace Free

The large and stalwart soul is on familiar terms with the mighty acts of God, set loose through the gifts of forgiveness, grace, and mercy.

The compassionate heart belongs to a person who has known the forgiveness of God and is willing to extend that forgiveness to another person.

The wise and aware human being realizes that there is nothing one person has done that he is not also capable of doing, given the same circumstances. The humble person understands the depth of the words "There, but for the grace of God, go I."

The psalms provide the words for confession. They provide the language for asking forgiveness. They give us a way to let go of what we did but shouldn't have done, to ask for mercy for the things we should have done but didn't do. They provide a way to help us deal with what has been done to us, and all of this happens under the sheltering arm of the God of compassion, patience, mercy, and grace. We pray for mercy to the God whose name is Love.

In the psalms, there is no place to hide our sin. It is laid bare before God, who sees all. In the psalms, there is no need to hide, for life is lived in the intimacy of a dynamic, personal, vital love relationship with God, who longs for the wholeness, health, and salvation of all his children.

By praying the psalms, we pray for our own brokenness and alienation. We pray for the healing of our guilt and the deliverance from our separation from God. We pray for the attitudes that separate us from God, and we pray for forgiveness for the actions that spring from these attitudes. We pray, as well, for others known and unknown to us.

Psalm 51:1

This is the great penitential psalm, the confession of one who has been driven, by his own choices and deeds, to the depths of despair and humiliation. It is the prayer for mercy in spite of one's guilt.

This is not the psalm to pray when you are saying, "Oh, excuse me," or "I was just kidding." This is not the prayer of cheap or easy grace, flippantly tossed to an indulgent parent who tends to let things go and look the other way.

This is the prayer of a penitent heart, a heart driven to its extremity by the knowledge of the harm that has been done. This is a prayer of one who will not hide behind excuses or rationalizations. This penitent says, "I did it. No one made me do it. I accept full responsibility for what I did and for the consequences."

It is also the prayer of the penitent who is on intimate enough terms with the Almighty that he knows where to go for forgiveness. This is a person who knows God well enough to have the freedom to ask for mercy.

In the stillness of this serious business of confession, go deeply within your heart and meet the God of mercy. Sit in the presence of the Holy One until all that is unholy in you can be brought into the light.

Do a fearless, searching moral inventory of your life. Hold nothing back from your own awareness. Be willing to face your own wrongdoing. Call it by its real name. Tell yourself the complete and unvarnished truth about what you've done.

Meet God's unfailing love in the confessional booth of your own heart. Speak the truth.

Psalm 51:2

DAY TWO

What is sin, anyway?

Sin is the condition of separation from God. It is the state of being disconnected, alienated, cut off from the presence of God. Sometimes we humans drift into that state of separation from God; sometimes we willfully choose to look into the face of God and defy him. We choose to go our own way, to think that we make the rules, to assume that we are in control.

In that state of alienation from the Source, we are motivated by the sins of attitude, those inner demons of fear, shame, guilt, hate, anger, inferiority, and inadequacy. We wear many masks to cover these afflictive and defeating emotions, but they are at work somewhere in the shadowlands of the soul, wreaking their havoc and making us do the things we don't want to do and not do the things we want to do.

From that inner motivation of alienation, fueled by afflictive emotions, we commit the deeds that match the belief. We say the words that wound and destroy. We behave in ways that injure ourselves and others. We commit the sins of action that wreck our lives.

In the silence, move into the innermost realm of your heart, that Holy of Holies where you and God speak only truth to each other. Confess to God all that you need to confess—your willfulness, your sins of attitude, and your sins of behavior.

In the silence, ask God to do for you what you cannot do for yourself.

If you are not yet willing to be forgiven, or if you are not yet willing to give up your favorite sin, ask God to make you willing to be willing. This is serious business.

The truth is that your very life may depend on the mercy of God. Do you live as if that is true?

159

Psalm 51:3-6

Whether you are doing a fearless, searching moral inventory or confessing the sin of the day, realize that you are going through this process in the context of a relationship with God, who is merciful and loving. God is not indulgent, but he is merciful.

When you go into a process like this, your concept of God will determine whether or not you can receive the grace of God and move on with your life. An erroneous, unbiblical concept of God can keep you wallowing in false guilt or keep you confessing that which you have already confessed. And if you continue to feel guilty after confessing, you are confessing to the wrong God!

In the silence, then, ask God to draw near to you. State your sin, either of will, attitude, or action. Be clear and direct. Name the people you have harmed, starting with the harm you have done to yourself.

As you wait in the silence, acknowledge that no matter what you have done to anyone else, at the bottom of it all is your sin against God. When you have committed a sinful act, it is the result of being severed from relationship with God, and the primary reparation that needs to take place is between you and the Almighty.

Feel the sorrow of contaminating your relationship with God.

Let yourself know that you have violated the covenant relationship with God. Feel the full impact of what you have done.

Give up blame. Stop making excuses. Don't hide out in victim language and don't say the devil made you do it. Stand up and admit the truth of what you have done.

Make your confessions first to God. Then ask God what to do about making amends.

Psalm 51:7-9

On this day, begin your season of silence by spending time focusing your attention on the presence of God within you and around you.

Reaffirm the nature of God, whose name is Love. Remind yourself that all discipline of God is to teach you the way of being right with God. Remember that the wrath of God is always bringing you back to where you ought to be. God's punishment is not about beating you up; instead, God works in the awfulness of your behavior to bring you to salvation and wholeness. God's mercy is redemptive, and God is full of compassion and love.

In the silence, let the words of this passage wash over you. Repeat them several times. Bring to mind the ways that your choices have affected your body and your life. Be willing to own the logical consequences of what you have done. Admit the truth that we are more often punished *by* our sins than *for* them. Be an adult and take responsibility.

Moving more deeply into the silence, dare to pray with all barriers down. Dare to ask God to move within your life and do what it takes to repair what you have broken. Be willing to be a part of that restoration.

In order to give God room to repair the damage, you will have to know where to relinquish your need to control and fix. You may have to lay down your need to protect yourself and others from the full impact of your choices. You may have to tolerate the discomfort of the process of restoration.

Keep the outcome in mind. Know that you will hear joy and gladness again.

Are you hurting enough to give God the freedom to do whatever God needs to do?

Psalm 51:10-12

Only the person who has been to the wrestling mat with his own self-will understands that it is not enough just to confess a sin or admit a character defect. Nature abhors a vacuum, and into that space where the sinful way or the sinful attitude once dwelled, a pure heart and a steadfast spirit must enter.

Only the person who understands that recovery or sobriety or serenity are fragile understands that every morning, she must begin again, choosing to live steadfastly. Only the person who has truly experienced God's mercy knows that God is the source of mercy and forgiveness and that asking for it is the way to receive it.

In the quietness of your own heart, invite God into that deep space where only you and he abide. Breathe deeply, affirming the presence of God within you. Acknowledge your dependence on the Lord of life and breath.

As you inhale, imagine that God is giving you the pure heart and steadfast spirit that you need to go about your day in grace and mercy.

As you exhale, release all that would keep God from keeping you steadfast.

Inhale, imagining the Holy Spirit dwelling within you, breathing new life into you.

Exhale, letting go of the dark spirits that break your body and wound your life.

Inhale, breathing in the joy of God's life within you.

Exhale, breathing out all resistance to God's restoring and strengthening work.

Inhale, affirming your willingness to let go and let God heal you.

Exhale, letting go and letting God.

Forgiveness and restoration are inside jobs. How much will you let God do within you?

Psalm 51:13-15

On this day, remember the ways you tried to take care of your sin on your own, by your own means, and within the limitations of your own resources.

Have you tried do penance? Does making amends do what you need?

Have you lived as if you are on parole, or as if you have been given a full pardon?

Are you living within the grace you have been given, or are you thinking you should be punished more? That which is not truly forgiven is often punished.

Have you made a habit of living in guilt, that afflictive feeling about something you have done? And is it false guilt or true guilt? Do you think another crucifixion would be enough, or was Calvary big enough for you—even you?

Do you live in shame, that afflictive emotion about who you are?

If you have been set free from the bondage of separation from God, who needs to know it?

Does your life reflect the grace you have been given?

In the silence, reflect on what you bring to your community of faith, your family, and your workplace as a result of having been forgiven.

Are you aware of the ways that your inner state affects the world in which you move?

Are you aware that the things you don't work through or discuss, you will project or take out on someone else? Do you work out your own stuff on other people?

Forgiveness, or the lack of forgiveness, has wide implications for the world in which you live.

Psalm 51:16-19

DAY SEVEN

Blessed are the poor in spirit, for theirs is the kingdom of heaven;
Blessed are those who mourn, for they shall be comforted.

—Matthew 5:3-4

In Japan, when a pot is fired and breaks in the process, it is not discarded. Instead, gold seals it back together. Pure gold is poured into the broken places.

When you are brought to your knees by the reality of what you have done and what you have left undone, you are in a good place. Then healing can begin.

When you have been broken open and are almost breathless in the pain of humiliation, embarrassment, and regret, you are in a good place.

When there is absolutely nothing you can do to repair the damage from your choices, and when you are face-to-face with the inevitable, you are in a good place.

When you are driven to the end of your rope and you have no more chances, that is the time when God can work best.

In the silence, bring that broken spirit to God and wait.

In the stillness, see yourself giving your broken and contrite heart to God.

Feel the despair. Own the anguish. Confess your need to God.

Grieve the loss of your innocence. Weep the sorrow of falling from grace in your own eyes and in the eyes of your loved ones. Admit your sin.

In the silence, imagine that God is moving toward you to pour a healing ointment into the cracked places of your heart. Whatever God does, he does well. His healing is the healing of pure gold. Let it wash over you. Let it heal your wounds.

Can you think of any reason that God would withhold his forgiveness?

Psalm 32:1-2

DAY ONE

"When you have truly accepted the forgiveness of God," a great person told me, "you can never forget it. You know what it cost you, and you know what it cost God."

This is a psalm to help you remember that you have been forgiven. It is a psalm of remembering, not to torture yourself or to afflict yourself with guilt again, but to remind you of the grace-gift you have received.

In the silence, recall that moment when you let forgiveness into your heart. If you need to, go back to the moment of confession and remember how good it felt to come clean before God. If you want to, go even further back to the moment of recognition of the gravity of your separation from God and the behavior that followed. Recall it only so that you can give thanks.

Let yourself sit in that holy place of grace and mercy. Feel again the blessedness of knowing that there aren't any barriers of unconfessed sin between you and God. Feel the joy of your clean, clear conscience before God.

Move your focus around the circle of your friends and family. Is there someone you know who cannot accept forgiveness or give it? Pray this psalm for that person.

Remember the terrible cycle of crime and punishment that begets more crime. Contrast the state of darkness with the state of blessedness. Pray for those who are locked in the cycle of guilt and do not know the way out. Pray for those who do not know their own separation from God. Pray for those who have no one to pray for them.

Are you willing to be an instrument of God's grace in the world? Are you open to the challenge of radical forgiveness—of practicing it, living it, giving it?

Psalm 32:3

DAY TWO

Guilt has to go somewhere. Plunged beneath the level of conscious awareness, it grows like a fungus. What is buried alive stays alive. Guilt often comes out in a physical symptom or a relational difficulty. Guilt demands attention, one way or another.

Unconfessed sin creates barriers between God and the very people God wants to forgive. Often, the only way a person knows how to deal with the shadow in his heart and soul is to project it onto someone else, making someone else carry his shadow.

In the silence of today, scan your life and remember what it was like when you kept your darkness outside your own awareness. Remember the dull ache of that thing you cannot face. Recall how much energy it took to hide your sin from God or yourself. What about the defense mechanisms you created to act as fig leaves for hiding yourself from God?

If you have come through that hiding-out time and have come clean before God, give thanks for grace.

If there is still unconfessed sin, be assured that it will manifest itself in some way. What you do not face in your inner life, you will often face in your outer world.

Remember the times when you have made confession. Make a decision to come clean before God at the end of every day. Don't let your account stack up with him, once you've made your big confession. Keep your accounts current with God and other people. Make amends quickly. And then, live in grace.

Who do you need to forgive? Whose forgiveness do you need? What's stopping you?

166

Psalm 32:4-5

How do you experience the heavy hand of God?

Do you know when God is pursuing you, showing you where you are out of alignment with him or out of integrity with yourself?

Is your connection with God intimate enough that you know immediately when you have hurt someone, either intentionally or unintentionally?

Or have you walked in the old self-defeating patterns so long that they feel natural?

Have you done the same destructive things so long that you no longer notice feeling bad? Have you detached yourself so thoroughly, and for so long, from the heart of God that your soul has become calloused?

Have you ignored the beckonings of God for so long that it feels like God has finally left you alone?

In the silence, acknowledge the times when you have turned down your own path, ignoring the inner voice of God. Remember the ways and means he has had of getting your attention and bringing you back to the place you are supposed to be.

It is good to have the spiritual sensitivity to know when God pursues you. It is good to be aware enough to know when you have acted outside the boundaries of God's loving permission. It is healthy to know that you have offended God and hurt someone else by a word, a thought, or a deed. Be glad when you know that you have hurt another person by that thing you have left undone.

You and God are in a covenant relationship, remember? He wants you to hear him speaking to you just as much as you want him to listen to you when you call on him!

Psalm 32:6-7

The LORD your God is with you,
he is mighty to save.
He will take great delight in you,
he will quiet you with his love.
He will rejoice over you with singing.

—Zephaniah 3:17

Who is this God who *sings?*

What are the "songs of deliverance"? And how can you hear them?

The psalmist makes the way clear. He knows how to activate the songs of God, songs that will come in the most surprising ways to keep you on the level path. God's music breaks through when you have made a good confession.

One day, it may be a friend who shows up, like a visible song, to encourage you and keep you on your path. You may see something in nature so beautiful that you experience it as the music of God, and you are strengthened by the sight of it.

On another day, the song of God may come in the form of a book that shows up at just the right time. It may come as a coincidence, a meaningful connection of events in a way that transcends logical explanation. Sometimes, the words of an actual song may seem to jump out of a radio and grasp your mind and heart. Now and then, a memory rushes into your conscious mind at just the right moment, reminding you of what God has done for you in the past. In those delightful synchronicities, God is at work, singing songs of deliverance to help you on your path.

While you are still and quiet, open your mind and heart to hear the songs of God.

Psalm 32:1

Count on it. You can rely on God, the Teacher. The Counselor is faithful and consistent.

The psalmist's faithfulness to God is greeted by a promise from God. As the psalmist perseveres in the life with God, God speaks a promise to him. This is what God told the psalmist; this is what we can expect from God.

Today, sit with your palms open in your lap. Let your open hands be a symbol to you and to God of your open mind and heart. Your hands are a silent prayer, a body prayer. They are a statement of your willingness to be led and taught by God.

As you remain in the silence, be open to hearing the guidance and instruction of God in any way that God decides to give it to you.

Admit that you don't know how God will speak. Acknowledge that God might want to speak to you in a way that he has never spoken before. Don't box God in the past or in conventional ways. He might have something new to try on you, something designed just for you.

Instructions often follow an act of confession. Confession acts like the removal of trash from a well. Getting rid of the debris of the soul makes it possible for the fresh, living water of God to flow smoothly into your consciousness.

As you remain in the silence, remember that when God speaks, it is up to you to follow. It is his job to guide you. It is your job to trust and obey.

Obedience is the hallmark of a trusting heart. A forgiven heart trusts more easily.

Has God given you guidance lately? Did you follow it? If not, why not?

Psalm 32:9-10

You cannot choose up and down at the same time. You cannot choose darkness and light, blessing and curse, life and death at the same time.

At the beginning of the day, recognize your human tendency toward willfulness. Acknowledge that your willfulness has led you to places you shouldn't have gone. Remember the difficulties you have caused by your own self-will.

Within each moment, you have a choice. You can live in the state of grace that you have been given because of the great forgiveness of a merciful and loving God. You can choose to trust God and let his unfailing love be the source of your life. You have the freedom to choose that way of life, a way that is life-giving, life-affirming, life-supportive.

You can choose the way of stubbornness. You can balk at the guidance of God. You can, if you choose, walk yourself right back into a hell on earth by the power of your own free will. It is your decision, day by day, moment by moment, and breath by breath.

Know that you have the choice, and then make the choice to live. Think ahead to the various challenges of your day and pre-decide to choose life. Think ahead to the challenges that you can't even see, dangers and risks that lurk around the corner, especially when you think you've arrived and don't have to depend on God for your guidance. At the beginning of the day, decide how you are going to live this day.

If you blow it by noontime, or even before, go back to that deciding point and re-decide. With God, you get chance after chance.

Choose God. Choose forgiveness and mercy. Choose love. Choose life.

What will you choose for yourself? As you choose, the way will open.

Psalm 32:11

On a little table beside the chair where I practice the discipline of silence, there is a special brass paperweight. It is made in the shape of the Hebrew symbol for *life*.

Every time I choose to receive forgiveness or give forgiveness, I choose life. Every time I practice the sacred art of forgiveness, I affirm the life-giving activity of God, the author and finisher of every act of forgiveness. Each time I choose to live in radical forgiveness, I participate with God in restoring life.

Such an amazing thing as forgiveness surely requires a declaration of praise and thanksgiving. Surely, being set free from the chains of the sin of separation deserves an affirmation of gladness! The costly grace of redemption demands a response to the Giver of redemption!

In the silence, give thanks for the forgiveness of God extended toward you. Be specific. Name the times God has bought you back and brought you back to his heart.

In the quiet, name the people who have forgiven you. Give thanks that, though they could have gotten even or taken revenge, they chose to give you mercy.

In this holy space, pray for those who live in the terrible grips of revenge and the deadly need to get even. Pray for those who bear a grudge or carry a chip on their shoulders. Pray for those who are victims; pray especially for those who play the victim, locked in the deadly jaws of the need to be pitied, the yearning to be martyred, the tendency to play "kick me."

Pray for the grace to be the kind of person who sets grace free!

When was the last time you gave thanks for the deliverance of God? Do it now!

Psalm 38:1-4

DAY ONE

If you live long enough, life is going to happen to you.

Unless you hide out in a bunker somewhere, isolated from other human beings, you are going to experience life's struggles. You will experience conflict. You may even experience estrangement from the people you love most. The more deeply you are involved with other human beings, the more you will be faced with the need to forgive and be forgiven. Sometimes, our conflicts with other people make us sick.

Someday, you will know the anguish of physical suffering. You will either see it or you will experience illness, because it is part of the human condition. Sometimes, physical, spiritual, and emotional suffering are interconnected. Now and then, the suffering of the soul and the agony of guilt are all the same thing, and they are manifested in physical symptoms.

Pray this psalm when guilt turns inward and wracks your body with pain and suffering. Pray this psalm when the results of your deeds and the regret of unconfessed sin or unresolved conflicts come home to the body, where they are trapped and experienced as excruciating pain.

Pray this psalm when what you have done is so big that your body hurts. Regardless of the cause, this pain feels like the punishment of God, and that is a terrible thing.

Is this prayer for you? Do you know this kind of suffering? If so, rest in this psalm. Pray it until it prays in you. Turn to it and let it become your prayer.

This is the prayer when your suffering is unbearable. This is the psalm of desperation.

Psalm 38:5-8

What do you do when someone has done something to you that has hurt you and harmed the relationship, and the other person won't attempt to work things out with you?

What about that terrible pain when you have done something to hurt someone else, and they will not forgive you? What do you do when you have owned your part of the problem, made amends and done everything you can do to repair the damage, and the person has closed the door of his heart and will not allow you back in?

What happens when someone keeps doing the same thing to you? How do you handle a relationship when another person makes you the scapegoat or takes out her anger on you, anger that belongs to someone else?

When you have been used or abused by another and forced to admit that the person hurt you knowingly, intentionally, and repeatedly, what is the work of forgiveness? What do you do when another person refuses to see or acknowledge his part of the estrangement?

As you examine your own heart and motivations in intimate relationships, where is the redemptive energy of forgiveness stuck? Who blocks the healing power of grace and mercy? What is your part in keeping a grudge alive? Is staying locked in the conflict the only way you know to deal with what is wrong between you?

Pray this psalm for others trapped in the prison of nonforgiveness. Pray this psalm on behalf of those who cannot or will not pray it for themselves. Pray it for the part of you that is unwilling to forgive. Pray it and weep.

Psalm 38:9-10

In the stillness of this holy space, and as you read this psalm, know that you are standing on holy ground when you do the work of forgiveness. In this space, the space made holy because of the presence of God and God's redemptive initiative toward us, you partner with God in the delicate work of mercy and grace.

Ask the Spirit of Truth to scan your heart and mind. Ask God to beam the searchlight of Truth into your motivations and your methods, your desires and your behaviors. Let God guide you to see what is in your heart.

Become willing to bring your mixed motives into the light of Truth. Agree with God about the desires of your heart, the desires you would prefer to hide from him and from yourself. Allow God to reveal everything in you that comes between you and God and you and other people.

Of course, your heart will pound with the knowledge of your shadow. Naturally, you will be uncomfortable with the Truth about your mixed motives and, worse, your selfish and mean motives.

Remember, however, that you open your heart before the One who loves you and longs for your wholeness. The One at work in you, attempting to bring you to health, wholeness, and salvation, is with you in the hard road of getting honest. The Spirit of Truth leads you to the truth and helps you tell the truth, starting with yourself. You will feel so much better when you say what is true.

Go ahead, get your longings out in the open. This time, dare to say what you want. Take responsibility for what was behind that hurtful thing you did.

Psalm 38:11

We are asked to extend two hands of forgiveness in our intimate relationships where there is conflict. We hold out a hand that says, "I'm reaching out to you as a gesture of my openness to reconciliation."

There is another hand, however, held in the gesture of "Stop!" that says, "You will never treat me this way again. The patterns must change."

The problem in processes of forgiveness is that we forgive and forget, which leaves the door open for repetitive patterns of abuse. Part of the mighty work of forgiveness is the conscious and aware *remembering* of the destructive patterns—not so you can hold a grudge, but so you can change the patterns! We must remember enough to stop the habits that hurt.

In these verses, we remember that the harm we do affects our lives with others. Our destructive patterns contaminate the processes between us. We impose our "stuff" on others. In nonverbal ways outside our awareness, we ask others to pay for our sins, to carry our projections and work out our anger and fear.

Praying this psalm, ask to know how to live in a new way, the way of radical forgiveness, with the people who are most important to you. Ask for the strength to insist on clean and clear interactions. Ask for the God of mercy to help you help him in setting yourself and others free from the disruptive ways of dysfunctional habits.

Who is your problem, that person who "gets you"? What are you learning about yourself from that person? And to whom are you a problem?

Psalm 38:12-16

My father used to tell me, "Don't explain. Your friends don't need it, and the others won't understand or accept it, anyway."

Was he right? Does that principle work in all situations? Or must I be accountable in certain circumstances?

It's hard when others question your motivation. It's tough when others set you up to put you down. It's difficult when you know there are people who would love to see you fail and who exult in bad news about you.

Pray this psalm when you have been wounded or falsely accused. Pray this psalm when others are looking on the outside and cannot see the agony and suffering on the inside of your life.

In the silence, confess the agony of being misjudged and misunderstood. If you can, offer the kind of forgiveness that says, "I forgive you, for you don't know what you do." If you aren't there yet, can you pray for the willingness to get there? Can you stand, convinced of your own motivations, letting people have their own interpretations of you? Can you give up the need to control what other people think of you? Can you give up your obsessive need to be understood and accepted?

While you're in this sacred space, go ahead and take a look at your life and notice where you might be out of integrity. Notice those places where there is a discrepancy between what is on the inside and what you present to the world.

Ultimately, you answer to God and your own integrity. In the meantime, you still live in the world of others' interpretations of you. How will you handle this?

Psalm 38:17-20

Pray this psalm when you are truly in desperate circumstances. Pray it when you are sick, or when you are sick and tired of being sick and tired. It is the "end of the rope" prayer, when you cannot muster the strength to take the next step. It is for those times when dying would be so much easier than living. Pray this psalm for yourself, and pray it for those who are sick. Pray it for those who cannot pray for themselves. You don't have to know every detail of another's suffering to pray this psalm; pray it on behalf of those who suffer.

Now and then, you may need this psalm for the occasions when your despair is compounded by what others think or how others treat you. It is for the true victim, and not the one who plays the victim. This is the prayer for the times when you have been asked to carry what does not belong to you.

A strange and perverse twist of human nature is our need to scapegoat other people. Families need "the problem child," the child who carries the negative energy of the family. Cultures need "the enemy" on which they can place their darkness. People somehow "need" a scapegoat on whom they can lay the iniquities of their own sins.

Move deeply into the silence and tread carefully in this terrible place. Dare to ask God for the stark, unvarnished truth. How does God want you to see yourself and other people? Are you carrying the shadow of others? Worse, are you the one who scapegoats another, causing that person unbearable anguish?

If you truly want to live in radical forgiveness, everything must come out in the open.

Psalm 38:21

DAY SEVEN

In the same way, the Spirit helps us in our weakness. We do not know what we ought to pray for, but the Spirit himself intercedes for us with groans that words cannot express.

—Romans 8:26

Driven to the extremities of our abilities, we often don't have the strength to articulate exactly what we want or need to say.

Pushed to the end of our strength, we can't even get to prayers for justice and righteousness. At the end of our ability to tolerate the pain any longer, we cry out for deliverance. Eventually, all of us need the One who will simply take away the pain.

Sometimes, we need a Rescuer, and we need one fast. Sometimes, all we can pray is "Help!" Now and then, we are in such despair that all we can do is breathe and hope God will hear the prayer of our hearts.

In the silence, pray these lines. Memorize them so they will come to you when you need them.

Call to remembrance those who suffer. Pray for those who suffer from the pain they have inflicted on others or on themselves. Pray for those who are wounded by the heinous acts of others. Pray for those you know and those you do not know. Pray this prayer for the human family.

Pray this prayer for the worst criminals. Pray it for those who will not see their own sin. Pray it for those with unrepentant hearts. Pray it for the part of you that will not repent.

What in your life is too hard for you to handle? Pray this psalm for that part of you.

178

Gratitude: The High Road of Faith

There is a powerful secret to serenity and peace on the spiritual path, and the secret is found in the consistent, daily practice of gratitude. People who have been to the depths of despair know that staying in true and sincere gratitude is one of the primary ways to stay grounded and centered. It's a discipline worth cultivating.

Perhaps you have had the experience of preparing a celebration of someone's big event, and they took it for granted or hardly seemed to notice your weeks of hard work. Maybe you have given a gift—an actual material gift or the priceless gift of your time, your attention, or your love—to another, only to have it ignored or spurned. What good parent doesn't know the disappointment of not hearing "thank you" from a child?

Gratitude is the act of remembering the Source of the blessings. Giving thanks keeps humility alive, for it takes the origin of your blessings away from your own efforts and places it on the One who truly is the giver of all good things.

Gratitude is preventative. It chases away self-pity and negativism. Cultivating an appreciative attitude helps you see the small gifts, day by day, and keeps your focus on what you have instead of what you don't have. Gratitude simply helps you see better.

Noticing what God has done and giving thanks for it has a way of enlarging your capacity to embrace God's bounty, which is everywhere. Gratitude is a habit of the surrendered heart. It is the way of peace and of overcoming, a large step toward freedom. The Psalms show the way to incorporate gratitude into life.

What God wants is a "thank you." How hard could that be?

Psalm 66:1-4

What is it about praising God and giving thanks that is good for you? Does your praise come from your heart? Is it filled with passion and love, or is it a mental exercise?

Temperaments differ, and so do expressions of praise and thanksgiving. No one can judge from the outside the sincerity of another's worship. Emotionalism and sentimentality may not be the same as true joy and thanksgiving. We each must search our own hearts, and each of us has the freedom, the opportunity, and the right to express thanksgiving in our own ways.

In the silence of this holy space, assess your way of giving thanks to God. More important than how high you can jump or how loudly you can shout are how straight you can walk and how honestly you can speak. Only you and God know the quality of your thanksgiving and praise.

In your inner sanctuary, meet God. In any way that works for you, imagine God is with you.

As you repeat the verses for today, say them slowly. Speak them as loudly or as quietly as you choose. Let the "shouting" be the depth of sincerity; let the sound you make come from the integrity of your own life.

Waiting in the silence, let the awesome deeds of God come to you, one at a time. As those gifts come to you, give thanks in your own way.

Affirm that all of creation is sustained by God. That includes you.

God accepts the praise from your heart, expressed in the manner that is right for you.

Psalm 66:5-7

When something good happens to you, don't you want to tell someone about it?

When you know that God has done something good for you, do you want to give God the credit?

Do you hesitate to talk about the goodness of God, fearing that someone will consider you a religious fanatic? Are you shy about attributing some gracious gift to God? You don't mind showing what a loved one has given you for Christmas, do you?

Or do you speak religious talk so much that you water down the mighty acts of God? Do you trivialize your life with God by making conversations about the Almighty so commonplace that they lose their impact? It's hard to find a balance sometimes.

Today, let yourself know first of all what awesome works God has done on your behalf, and if you cannot identify those works, take extra time to be still and know. Become willing to see how God has graced your life. Look around you and within you and recognize the hand of God.

As you move more deeply into the silence, ask yourself how long it has been since you gave God credit for what you have. How long has it been since you shared God's goodness in your life with a family member? a friend? a coworker? the person you sit by in worship?

Do you ever take God for granted, receiving the bounty from his good hand and heart but not taking the time to thank him?

What kind of friend to God are you, anyway?

How long has it been since you've updated your gratitude journal?

Psalm 66:8-9

It's spiritually healthy to give thanks to God in the privacy of your inner sanctuary. Giving thanks for your personal blessings is an important discipline, and the more you do it, the more you will benefit from the practice.

There is also value in praising and thanking God corporately. Acknowledging the blessings of God often calls for group praise. Telling other people within your faith community what God has done for you inspires the faith of others.

For today, consider the interrelatedness of your personal faith journey and the journey of your community of faith. How does each enhance the other?

In what ways are you "carrying your load" within your faith community? Do you give praise where praise is due, or do you keep quiet about the blessings of God?

Who within your faith community stirs up your faith? Who feels encouragement in his life with God because of your faith practices?

Do the children within your faith community know the stories of God's goodness? Do they know the heroes of faith who have lived among you? Are they aware of the ways in which God has preserved your lives and kept you from slipping?

Is your life a living affirmation of the presence of God? If you know the joy of God within you, can anyone else see it? Does your work reflect an attitude of thanksgiving? Do your relationships manifest an awareness of the presence and activity of the grace of God?

What might God be asking you to do/say/be in order to witness to the hope within you?

Psalm 66:10-12

DAY FOUR

Life is not perfect. Any day has its mixture of ups and downs.

God is just as present in difficulty as he is in blessing—if we learn to see with eyes of faith. Thanksgiving sharpens focus. As you reflect on these verses, look back at the hard times in your life. Remember when you didn't know what to do and you couldn't find your way. Can you identify the lessons you learned?

Reflect on the times when you failed or lost something that meant a lot to you. While you might not be able to find something positive in any of those experiences, can you see where God was with you?

What about the time you railed against God, when you were given a big disappointment or a burden you thought you could not bear? Is there a time when what you thought was a burden turned out to be a blessing in disguise? If so, what finally made you able to see the blessing?

What about those times when you were tested by the fires of life, times when you didn't know if you would come out of the fire as cinder or silver? Can you identify elements of the testing that you now know were necessary for growth and development? Have you thanked God for those times?

And have you experienced an outright miracle from the hand of God? Has something worked out in your life that could not possibly have worked out without the direct intervention of God? Have you told that story to anyone? Do you take the credit, or do you recognize the Source?

Do the people in your community of faith know how God has blessed you?

Psalm 66:13–15

"God has done so much for me that I am going to spend the rest of my life showing my appreciation by serving him."

"I have been blessed so richly by God that I must do something to show him how grateful I am."

"I am a person of privilege. How can I not give back to the world? How else can I show God how thankful I am?"

God does not require us to sacrifice animals, so what is the appropriate response to the goodness of God?

Without consistent acts of gratitude, whether voiced in song, prayer, or the silent praise within one's own heart, it's easy to forget the Source of life. With forgetting comes a feeling of entitlement, as if one somehow deserves the blessings and benefits of the privileged.

In the inner prayer room, where only you and God meet, open your mind and heart to hearing the guidance of God. Ask God to show you an appropriate response to your blessings.

The acts done to express appreciation to God are not about earning points with God. They aren't about impressing others. Responding to the bounty of God in some specific act of response is not about building a hedge of protection around your life or bargaining with God in any way.

What is the appropriate response to the goodness of God in your life? What does God ask of you in return for his blessings? How can you ever thank God enough for all he has done for you?

Psalm 66:16-20

In twelve-step groups around the world, people recovering from addictions gather on a regular basis to tell each other the miracles of their recovery. In fact, staying sober—either emotionally or physically—requires an ongoing process of saying out loud and in public, "This is how I was. This is what God did. If God did this for me, he can do it for you."

Around the globe, recovering people meet with their sponsors, individuals who have worked the program for a long time and have experienced healing. Over coffee or over the telephone, often in the middle of the night, sponsors reaffirm the principles of the program that works. They give an account of the hope within them, and they hang in there with the one who is struggling until that person has a miracle story of his or her own.

Do you have a story of faith to tell another seeker? Who needs to hear it?

Have you looked closely enough at your history to know the moments when God broke through your experience to turn your life around? Who needs to know that?

Whose story would you like to know? Whose experience of the Living God is so vital and alive that you want to know how they have gotten there? Is it possible for you to ask that person what his experience of the Living God is, so that your own faith can be fanned into a burning flame, a flame around which others can gather for warmth and light?

God becomes alive for us in real ways as we tell about the mighty acts of God among us. Who needs to hear your story? Whose story do you want to hear? Do it!

Psalm 100

Go ahead. Make it a priority. Make it fervent. Make it regular and consistent. Make the faithful worship of God through praise and thanksgiving a part of your life.

Make your private times of praise, worship, and thanksgiving a priority in your everyday life. Do this and you *will* come to know that the Lord is God. Don't wait until you feel it to do it. Do it, and then the feeling will come.

Make corporate worship a priority in your life. Gather with your community of faith regularly so you can borrow from their faith when your bucket is empty. Give freely when your own bucket is full. Sing and say together the affirmations of faith; do it with your whole heart. Let your individual praise be a gift to your community of faith.

In the silence of this day, speak this psalm aloud. Sing it. Whisper it. Let its ancient words settle in your memory and in the recesses of your heart. Keep them near you for the entire day, calling them up wherever you are.

Linger over each line. Hold it in the silence for as long as you can and let the words speak to you. Learn what it means to enter the gates of God with thanksgiving!

Embrace this psalm so thoroughly that it begins to pray within you. Welcome it so intimately that it bubbles underneath your consciousness during the day. Wake up with it in the morning and go to sleep with it at night.

If you will be faithful to this psalm, you will come to know that you can enter the gates of the Lord, wherever you are.

As you own this psalm, you will know from now on that the Lord is good and that his love endures forever.

Psalm 136

DAY ONE

On this day, push back all of the boundaries of your mind and seek the big picture.

In the stillness, let the ancient words resound in your own mind, over and over: *God's love endures forever.* Say them slowly. Linger over them.

As you read this litany of praise and thanksgiving, move back and forth between the mighty acts of God in history and the acts of God in your own life.

Continue to affirm, *God's love endures forever.* Let the words follow your breathing.

Let your affirmation of that which God has done in the past be a statement of trust in God's activity in the present and the future. Remind yourself that God's nature does not change. God's love endures forever.

Move your focus into the present moment. Look closely at what is right in front of you, enriching your life on this day. Imagine that your life is under a microscope. Look for the smallest gifts of God, and give thanks for them.

Pray this psalm when your heart overflows with gratitude for all that you have been given.

Pray this psalm when you feel disconnected from God, especially if it results from your forgetting the goodness of God extended toward you.

Pray this psalm when you feel discouraged and are tempted to slide into self-pity. Pray this psalm to keep yourself remembering Who is the Source of every good and perfect gift?

Who needs to hear your gratitude? How will you express it?

Psalm 24:1-2

Feeling a little arrogant? Think you've earned all of your blessings?

Are you down and depressed, afraid that God won't hand out any favors to you?

What made you lose the connection with God? Does the same thing separate you from God over and over?

Before you slide farther down the slippery slope away from God, move intentionally and quickly to this psalm. Let it serve as a corrective. It keeps you knowing Who is in charge, and you can relax.

In the silence, bring to mind the pictures of this planet, taken from the moon. Let your mind wander around the globe. See in your imagination the splendor of the mountains and the depths of the ocean. Recall the places you have seen that take your breath away with their beauty. Remember looking into the faces of your loved ones and seeing their loveliness.

Imagine that you can get a bird's eye view of your own world, the world you have built with your effort and skill. Recall your responsibilities. Think about the people who depend on you to do your work.

Move into the silence and affirm the lines for today's meditations. Let their wisdom fill your mind and heart with calmness and peace. Let them remind you who is the Creator and who is the creature. Give thanks that God is in charge of the world.

In God's order, God creates. Humankind is given the privilege of worshiping God, loving people, and using things. Life works best when we keep that order.

Is there a place in your life where you are using people and worshiping things?

Psalm 24:3-6

DAY THREE

What things occupy your mind and heart? Are they worthy of your time and attention? You are, after all, created in the very image of God. You are the temple of God, created just a little lower than the angels.

Today, ask God to move deeply into your inner life and bring to your consciousness the things that are not worthy of you.

Ask God to remove the things that separate you from him. Ask him to empty your mind of attachments that distract you from your purpose in life. Ask him to clear the disruptive emotional programming of a lifetime, programming that causes you to fear.

Within every self-defeating pattern, there is an emotional knot that has attached to it behaviors, thought patterns, beliefs, and emotions. Within that knot, there is a lie, a lie that was formed early in life. A knot in the soul takes up space in which the blessings of God cannot move.

Ask the Divine Therapist to move deeply into that knot and expose the lie. Cooperate with the process. Keep going back into the silence and offering that knot to God and trust that God is at work in that process. Give thanks for the possibility that such cleansing can happen. And when that knot and the lie are exposed, give thanks. Give it lavishly and fervently.

When you have experienced the healing process of the Divine Therapist, fill that void where the lie once was with the habit of gratitude. Give thanks for the deliverance of God. Give thanks that you can live in freedom. Give thanks that you, like the earth and all that is in it, belong to God.

What has God already done to heal you? Do you thank him every day for that?

Psalm 24:7-10

Press on!
—Louis Daniel Ball

Pray this psalm when you feel down and dejected. Pray it when your shoulders droop and you are depressed and discouraged.

Picture yourself lifting up your head! Put your shoulders back. Raise your eyes to the wonders of God! It's your choice. Choose praise and thanksgiving. Choose to glance at your problems, yes, but keep your gaze on the Lord Almighty.

Choose the high road, the road of faith and trust. Choose the path of God's strength and might. Give thanks for the presence of God, no matter what the externals of your life happen to be at this moment.

As you stay in the silence of this great psalm-prayer, ask God to empty your heart so that he can fill it with gratitude and praise.

Wait in the silence and see how God chooses to honor your gratitude and praise.

Continue to lift up your head until your spirits are lifted.

Pray this psalm for someone you know who has lost his way and does not remember that all things belong to God.

Pray this psalm for the one who cannot or will not give thanks.

Pray this psalm for the person who is dejected and depressed.

Let the words of this psalm be close to you, when you think you're in charge.

When you think the earth belongs to you, and that you are entitled to the blessings you've been given, what happens? Think it over and change your mind. You'll be glad you did.

190

Psalm 146:1-2

In the stillness of this time, recall the attributes of God that you see in the Psalms. Write them down. Put them in a place where you can find them easily, just in case you forget and start making God in your own image again. Bring those attributes of God to mind over and over until they become the predominant image of God you carry in your mind.

Perceiving God as God truly is praise to God.

List the other gods you have tried to make fill that hole in your soul. Put that list in a place where you won't lose it. Knowing the idols you are tempted to worship keeps you aware of your tendency. Include yourself on that list.

Giving only God the place of honor in your heart shows praise to God.

In the stillness, open your mind to ask the question, "What does it mean to praise God all your life?" Is there a way to make your whole life a praise to God, who made you? Can you imagine living your life as if God is your only audience? Can you bring all of your gifts, abilities, talents, and skills and offer them to God in an act of worship and praise, an act that acknowledges that every single thing you have comes from God?

Using your gifts as a gift to God shows praise to God, who gave the gifts.

Loving others toward God is a way of praising God. Forgiving others shows praise to God. Giving a cup of cold water in the name of God is a praise to God.

Is your life directed toward God or toward living your own way? Is it praise or drudgery?

Psalm 146:3-4

As you enter into the silence today, affirm the choice to live your life as if God is your only audience.

Remind yourself that God is present in this silent space.

Breathe deeply and affirm your commitment to the worship and praise of God.

Bring to mind your current biggest challenge. Who is involved with you in that challenge, either as ally or enemy?

As you bring to mind that person, ask yourself if you are depending on that person in an inappropriate or unrealistic way. Are you asking someone to do for you what you should be doing for yourself? Are you expecting someone to take care of you in a way that only God can? How does your unrealistic expectation contaminate your relationship with God or with that person?

Move your focus back to the presence of God, who is with you and in you. Reaffirm your love of God, and return your trust to the place where it belongs.

In the silence, give thanks that God is absolutely trustworthy.

Give thanks that God's love endures forever.

Give thanks that God's wisdom is perfect and that his ways are good.

Give thanks that God is good.

As you wait in the silence, be willing to see your life from the perspective of God. Open your mind and heart to the possibilities of seeing your life through the eyes of grace.

If you were God, what would you think of you? How would God introduce you?

Psalm 146

Today, take an inventory of your own unique and precious life, and give thanks for who you are.

Take an inventory of the skills you have developed and the natural abilities that you were given, and give thanks. All are gifts from God.

Notice the people who enhance your life. Pay special attention to the people who support your work or who help you in the practical or mundane activities. Who lights up your life? Who manifests God's love to you?

Think about the opportunities you have to learn, to stretch your mind, to experience the world. Can you give thanks for the challenges that cause you to see from a new perspective? Can you see that even in your difficulties, you have an opportunity to learn something new, to develop new strengths or to witness the activity of God in a new way that you didn't expect?

What do you enjoy about your temperament? What do you like about your way of relating to others, your particular style of problem-solving, your humor, or your capacity to feel with another person?

Take a look at the things in your life that are unfinished, incomplete, unsatisfying, or problematic. If you can't be thankful for those imperfections, can you at least find the gift of grace somewhere within them? Perhaps God has some kind of grace in the imperfection—if you are willing to look for it.

If you cannot yet be grateful for your own life, keep an open mind and heart to yourself.

Keeping the Faith

Getting Through Relapses

"Oh, no, I thought I was further along than this!" we wail when we stumble and fall over places we thought we'd conquered.

"I thought I had worked through this issue, but here it is, showing up in a different form!"

The spiritual journey is much like playing "Mother, May I." Sometimes, we take giant steps forward, and then, as soon as we do, we find ourselves going backwards. Often, after a particularly good retreat experience or a meditation that yields moments of ecstasy, we may get inflated. Quickly, life finds a way to deflate that pride and arrogance. And it is so hard to fall from grace in your own eyes!

In the Gospels, the failures often give us hope and courage. We look to the woman caught in adultery, the demoniac, the woman at the well, and the cursing, betraying Peter, and we see ourselves. Their imperfections help us know that the Living God wants to heal our own imperfections, restore us to wholeness, and transform us into new people. At the point of our inadequacies, the adequacy of God works best.

The psalms reveal a prayer life large enough to contain stumbling and falling. Praying the prayer book of Jesus, we come to see that the roller coaster of faith is allowed. No one has to "arrive." There are no special places for the spiritually elite.

The key in working through inevitable relapses is to get up, suit up, and show up for the next event. We accept the shadow in us as part of what it means to be fully human and fully alive. We acknowledge the darkness and the duplicity, the littleness and the stinginess. We also embrace the *imago dei* and we faith it forward, step by step.

Psalm 37:1–2

DAY ONE

It's tough to figure out what is your business and what is someone else's. Sometimes, it's even hard to know what is your business and what is God's!

In an instant, another person's tone of voice, choice of words, an intentional affront, or an inadvertent slight can shake you loose from your moorings and set your world spinning. Another person can get under your skin and on your nerves, destroying your equilibrium and carefully sought serenity or sobriety.

In the silence of today, create a space within your mind and let that space contain a stage. Ask yourself the question, "Who has the power to destroy my peace of mind?" and see who wanders across that stage.

Ask yourself, "To whom have I given the responsibility for my life, my happiness, my well-being?" Ask, "To whom have I given the power over my inner kingdom?" and "Who am I allowing to control me?"

Ask yourself, "Who is truly hurting me? How do I need to be wiser? How do I need to set better boundaries or protect myself in a better way?"

In the silence, make a decision to hold your center, that grounding place where you and God are connected. Use a prayer word as an anchor. Use your breathing to remind you that you and God are connected at the most intimate level of your life. Sometimes "Help me!" is all you need to turn a relapse around before it becomes a disaster. Give up fretting over what other people do. You *can* make that choice.

There is only One who has rights to your inner kingdom. There is only one God.

Psalm 37:3-4

Love the LORD your God with all your heart and with all your soul and with all your strength.

—Deuteronomy 6:5

The lines from the psalmist's heart contain wisdom that can change your life. Interpreted from a large perspective, they can be a corrective, an inspiration, or a guide. If you are lost, they can help you get back to the place you need to be. Think about this:

Trust in the Lord.

Do good.

Dwell . . . enjoy.

Delight yourself in the Lord.

If you have lost your way, or if you want to make good choice, let *these* commandments be your guide. If you are lost, you may need to try a different approach!

Bring to your imagination a picture of a time when you looked at a loved one with delight. Recall the feelings you had, delighting in the very being of another. Think about the pleasure you have in being with that person; experience the joy and love directed toward that person whom you can see and hear and touch.

In the silence of today, wonder about what it means to *delight* in the invisible God. What is it like to direct love and delight toward the Creator? How does it feel to imagine love streaming from your heart to the heart of God?

Delighting in God is the way back. Loving and trusting God brings your desires into alignment with God's desires for you. The delighting comes first, and then come the desires of your heart. Do you have it backwards, wanting your desires first?

Psalm 37:5-8

Move into today's meditation time with a commitment to take a fearless, searching moral inventory of your soul.

Move through these verses slowly, writing down each commandment. Leave space beside each one.

One by one, let each commandment guide you into self-knowledge. Find the places where your soul is stuck. Tell yourself the truth about where you are choosing your own way and trying to make it on your own, living out the frustrating life of a practical atheist, as if there is no God who longs to help you.

What part of your life have you not committed to him?

What part do you need to recommit to him?

What is God asking you to entrust to him?

Where are you rushing ahead of God, refusing to be still and wait for him?

Where are you focusing your attention on "evil men," the people who are doing things you don't like or those who are doing what you don't want them to do?

Where do you need to give up control?

What makes you mad? Where do you need to give up anger?

What are you fretting about? What would happen if you gave that up?

In the silence, wait and see what God wants you to know about yourself. If you are in a habit of being too hard on yourself, lighten up. If you are too lenient, get tough!

Where is God asking you to lead? to follow? to get out of his way?

Psalm 37:9-22

DAY FOUR

Create in your mind's eye a peaceful setting. Paint a picture of clear blue skies and green pastures. Feel a cool breeze on your face and the warmth of the sun on your shoulders. Smell the aromas of springtime. Hear the song of the birds and the sounds of a gentle stream. Taste the cool, clear water.

As you breathe deeply, reaffirm your connection to the Living God. Regardless of what is going on in your life, claim the power of the peace of God within your inner world. If your emotions won't coincide with this reality, allow them to be what they are. In the present moment, just *be*.

From this place of imagined peace and tranquillity, turn a laser beam on what bothers you in your outer world. Notice how that external thing tries to interrupt your inner calm. Perhaps that outer problem prevents your inner tranquillity.

Ask yourself questions, and be willing to hear the truth.

Where are you trying to take over God's business?

What is your business and what is the business of someone else?

Why is it so hard for you to mind your own business?

What do you need to do to discern the difference between the things you can change and the things you cannot change?

Who do you need to talk to about this issue?

Who can help you discern what is yours to handle and yours to release?

Do you trust God enough to let him handle what belongs to him? If not, why not?

Psalm 37:23-33

How do you get God to delight in your ways?

Go back to the first part of the psalm. Read again the commandments. Wake up to the reality that God works best for you when you carry out God's desires, instead of the other way around.

Get the order in mind, and hold it there. The way things work best is when God initiates the plan. The way you find out the plan for your life is to delight in God and to trust him with your efforts.

There is something farther back, however. The delight in God and love for God don't really start with us.

We love because God first loved us.
                              —John 4:19

In your imagination, picture yourself sitting with God in that pastoral scene you created yesterday. Look into the face of God and see his love for you. See how he delights in you, his unique creation. Notice how he looks at you with tenderness and compassion. Notice how he *delights* in you, his beloved child.

That is where it starts. God initiates the relationship through mysterious ways that human beings cannot even begin to understand. God starts the conversation. He reaches out to each person, extending love.

Hold that truth in your conscious mind. Return to it over and over. You are able to love God and delight in God because God has loved you first.

Say the truth. Speak it until you believe it. Speak it even when you don't believe it. Say it especially when you don't believe it. God loves you.

Psalm 37:34

Waiting for God is one of the hardest things we humans are asked to do, especially in a world of jet travel, microwave cooking, and internet communication.

Waiting for God is one of the hardest things capable people have to do. The more personal resources you have, the harder it is to let God work things out in the fullness of his timing.

We are required to wait during those times when there are no easy resolutions. This is the psalm for praying when waiting is the task and you need vigorous faithing skills, determined and undeterred hoping capabilities. And those are often the times you feel those things the least.

In the silence, bring your restless, impatient spirit to God and confess how you feel about his timing. Tell him how frustrated you are with his slow ways. Tell him how you feel about his taking his own, sweet time to do what you know he could do in a flash!

Confess it all, and then wait. Wait for God when you don't feel like waiting. Wait for God when you cannot see the next step to take.

Wait for God, but stay busy. Do what you can. Take care of yourself. Keep living your life, enjoying all that you can in every moment.

You don't have to know *how* God is going to act. All you need to know is *that* God will act. Don't look frantically about you, searching here and there for evidence of God's presence. Trust that God will show up. Keep your eyes and ears open.

What would it cost to ask God to give you passionate hope while you wait?

Psalm 37:35-40

This is the psalm about *ultimate* resolution.

It is not the psalm that gives false hope.

This is the psalm that gives guidance for how to behave when you've lost your way. It is not a formula for guaranteeing the success of your program and the failure of your enemy's.

This is the psalm to pray when you need to get that part of you that is righteous—the part that is in right relationship with God—in the driver's seat of your life, and the part of you that is evil—the part that wants to go your own way—out of the driver's seat. Both selves exist within you.

You know the part of you that is on God's side. That part has the humility to cooperate with God and is willing to acknowledge that this is, after all, God's world, and you are the one in service to the Almighty. You know, don't you, that true self, the self lined up with God?

You know that other part of you as well. You know that part of you that insists on your own way, the part that wants to please and placate others, the part that wants security and worldly favor, all at the expense of your soul?

Ultimately, God triumphs. Ignore the will of God at your own peril. This inner war of your ego or your adaptive self against your true self is the one you must address. Sooner is better than later.

Do you dare ask God to help you see the truth about your own many selves?

Psalm 16:1

Do you know yourself well enough to recognize the signs of an approaching relapse?

Can you sense when you are slipping into a state you don't want to be in?

Alcoholics call it "building up to drink," BUD, that state of being in which you're collecting feelings and experiences that will help you justify a binge.

You don't need alcohol or drugs to binge. You can binge on self-pity, worry, anger, depression, or fear. You can work yourself into a state of grandiosity or inflation. You can drown in your own feelings of worthlessness or inferiority. Dry drunks are different from alcoholic drunks, but they are devastating in their own way.

When you are sober, either emotionally or physically, take this verse and write in on the inside of your heart. Keep it close to you as a safeguard in those times when you are moving from the chair of faith onto the chair of disbelief.

In the silence, repeat the words as you inhale. *Keep me safe, O God.*

As you exhale, breathe out the next line. *For in you I take refuge.*

Repeat the words as many times as you need to—not as a formula, but as an anchor. Go to the inner refuge of God's presence—not as an escape, but as a place of gathering your strength and gaining the courage you need to live in the world.

Safety is not in any substance, person, or activity other than God. Safety is not to be found in any other god but the God of Love.

The gift of God's presence is peace. Ask God to grant you peace. Know that God desires to give you peace. Expect God to help you, breath by breath.

Practice taking refuge in God until it becomes natural to be with God. God is near.

Psalm 16:2-4

DAY TWO

As you wait in silence today, become aware of the dissonant voices in your head, voices that would nudge you toward defeat and discouragement. Notice the voices that urge you to follow the siren's song to a place where you don't want to be, a place where you allow lesser gods than the One who loves you to be in control of your will and your life.

Sometimes, you have only a split second between those thoughts and the behaviors that follow them. In that time, you have a choice, and one of the choices is to reach out for help. You can reach toward God and you can reach for one of God's helpers. They are out there, you know.

Who will be your support in your spiritual life? In the silence, allow your mind to know who is an advocate for your true self. Who is there to give encouragement to the part of you that wants to be whole and healthy?

Who are the people God has placed on your path to help you avoid relapses into self-will, fear, disbelief, and distrust? Who are the human instruments God is using to keep you on the path of faith, sobriety, serenity, and joy?

Are you willing to let someone know you well enough to know where you are prone to slip? Are you willing to call those people when you feel yourself slipping? Are you willing to ask for help when you have lost your way?

Are you able to know when it is "the next to the last straw"? Can you stop yourself from slipping by reaching out to someone who is willing to let you lean on his or her faith until you find your own footing again? Who are your personal saints?

Psalm 16:5-6

DAY THREE

If only you didn't have *that* particular character defect, right?

How much you could accomplish if you didn't have *that* thorn in the flesh? Why couldn't you have been given another one?

Did you really need *that* "blessing," a blessing that consumes your time and attention, demanding your energy and money?

Is it worth it, bearing *this* cross? And is this cross something God knows about? Did God know you would have *this* cross when he made you?

It is so easy to give thanks when things are going well and the blessings of God are rolling in. It is so hard to see the hand of God in the hard places. Sometimes, it takes a lifetime to recognize that the burden you bore for your time on this earth is the burden you needed to make you strong and capable and useful in the kingdom of God.

It's not always the case, but often, the boundaries we rail against are the ones that turn us toward God and make us secure. God somehow works in irony and paradox. Sometimes what seems to be burden is blessing, and what seems to be blessing is burden. Sometimes, it takes a lifetime to know the difference.

Acceptance seems to be the first step in keeping your balance and avoiding relapses. Sometimes, acceptance is the biggest and hardest challenge of a lifetime.

God, grant me the serenity to accept the things I cannot change,
the courage to change the things I can,
and the wisdom to know the difference.

—Reinhold Niebuhr

Psalm 16:7

DAY FOUR

What do you do with your dreams? Do you ignore them, chalking them up to the bad meal you had too late at night?

What if you began to take your dreams seriously, recording them in a journal and letting them speak to you?

Is it possible that your dreams have a message and that they are the soul's way of speaking to you in symbols when your defenses are down?

And what about your thoughts when you first wake up? Is it possible that those images and ideas are messages for you before your ego has a chance to get up and take charge of your conscious mind? When you are still in that in-between world, not quite awake and not quite asleep, the soul often speaks most clearly.

God *does* seem to have to use his own ways to get messages through. We are heavily defended against knowing the truth that lies within the deepest recesses of our hearts, and we are invested in the ego's way of being in the world. The ego is, after all, the organ of consciousness, and its job is to keep the status quo!

Today, let your mind drift back to dreams that might want to be honored and respected. Let your memory take you to those first thoughts of the day. Is it possible that God has been speaking to you all along, and you wouldn't listen?

In the silence, assess your willingness to be instructed in the night. In the amazing economy of the inner life, the unconscious seems to respond with the same respect it is given. If you believe God speaks through dreams and images, God will do that.

What keeps you defended against the messages from the kingdom within?

Psalm 16:8

Then, we will no longer be infants, tossed back and forth by the waves,
and blown here and there by every wind of teaching and by the cunning
and craftiness of men in their deceitful scheming.

—Ephesians 4:14

In the American culture, we humans love to bash our public figures if
they change their minds and cannot hold a position. We call it *waf-*
fling, and from our living rooms, we can spot waffling a mile away,
especially if it's on television.

In our own lives, we excuse that same activity and tendency in
ourselves, especially when it comes to the things of God. We make a
commitment to a discipline or to a recovery program, and then we are
so easily blown about by whatever comes along in the outer world.
The psalmist said what Paul affirms: Stand firm!

In today's meditation, speak the words of this verse as an affirmation. Picture in your mind what it means *for you,* in this present
moment, where you are, and with what you have to set before the
Lord.

Does it mean you are surrendered to God?

Does it mean you have turned your will over to God?

Does it mean you love God with all of your heart, mind, and
soul?

Does it mean you are seeking first the kingdom of God within
you?

Does it mean you are following God?

Does it mean you will go the distance with God, no matter what?

Does it mean you are committed to your life with God or to your
recovery?

You know what you can expect from God. What can God expect from you
on this day?

Psalm 16:9-10

Call unto me, and I will answer you and show you great and mighty things which you do not know.

—Jeremiah 33:3

How many times have you been in that moment when things could go either way with you and God? Are you aware enough of the ebb and flow of your own inner life to know when you teeter between the life of faith and the life of unfaith?

How often have you let go of that attachment to God and turned your attention to another god, only to know immediately that you should have kept your part of the covenant relationship?

God cannot do for a person what that person refuses to let God do.

Even God will not walk across the picket line of our defenses. God gives freedom of choice. *How do you choose, most of the time?*

Sobriety absolutely depends on the recovering person's choosing up instead of down, light instead of dark, life instead of death, moment by moment. Often, the recovering person's very life or death is dependent on that choice.

The seeker's serenity, peace, and power are absolutely dependent on choosing the high path as well. Moment by moment, the choice is made between love and fear. Over and over, the day or the character is made by the small choices, one by one.

In this day, savor these verses. Think about how God wants to be with you, and how much God loves you. Think of how much better life goes with God.

Choose God, over and over. Choose life, as many times as you need to choose it. Choose love. Choose grace. Choose mercy. Choose peace. Choose God. Do it again.

Psalm 16:11

Confused? Perplexed? Don't know which path to take?

Feeling overwhelmed? Thinking about twisting off, giving up, taking a break?

You've done all the right things, you say, and yet nothing seems to be working out like it's supposed to.

You've given and given to a person you love, and yet, the relationship keeps traveling south.

You read these ancient words. You wonder if they are meant only for the psalmist or for the most holy saints of God, but not for you.

You read that there is a plan for you life and that God knows what it is. Are you wondering if God is keeping the plan a secret from you?

As you enter the silence, "go within."

Take a risk. Take a deep breath. Turn your attention from the outer world and listen to the sounds in your own head.

You say it's chatter. You say you don't hear anything. You don't like what you do hear!

Take a risk. Take another deep breath. Stay with the silence. Expect God to guide you. God will speak. God will show you the path of life—if not in this moment, then at the moment when you can receive it.

When did God clearly speak to you, and you ignored it? Maybe you should apologize.

Psalm 19:1-6

When trouble comes, we think God has turned his back on us. In fact, we can look around and find all kinds of evidence to support the mistaken idea that God has abandoned his world.

Today, reconnect with nature. When you feel that God is absent, make time to see or touch or smell the natural world. Use your eyes and ears to appreciate the handiwork of God. Notice the evidence of *life* all around you. Let nature speak to you about the abiding presence of the Creator.

Take a walk and let each step be a silent affirmation of your connection to the Creator through the created world.

Sit beside big water or a big sky and contemplate the grandeur of God. Notice the design in a leaf or the patterns in the night sky and remember God's infinite ways of working in and through—and in spite of!—the natural world.

Look into the faces of strangers and loved ones and see each individual as a unique expression of the infinite creativity of God. Recognize that the God in you, the *imago dei*, is capable of connecting with the *imago dei* of another person. Claim your own life as the beloved child of God, and see that belovedness in the Other.

As you sit in the silence, breathe deeply. Affirm that God is literally bombarding your with love and with beauty through the natural world. Accept and embrace the fact that nature is God's gift to you. Let nature be God's gift to you.

How many of God's gifts do you miss as you rush around doing what you think is important?

Psalm 19:7-14

A spiritual relapse often starts with a stressful event, a change in schedule, a disturbing conversation, or a crisis. Something happens, and you regress to your earliest coping skills. The more stressful the stimulus, the more primitive the coping skill. "I acted like a child!" we say about ourselves. It's a shameful experience.

Sometimes a relapse occurs after you are soaring, going from glory to glory in your own process of recovery, whatever that is. Maybe you begin feeling a little too confident, a confidence that is born in the misbelief that you can accomplish spiritual growth on your own. Maybe you think, "I'll take today off!" and suddenly realize that you've slipped back into the old style of relying on your own resources instead of God's.

At other times, you may slip into a relapse when you feel that you have worked and worked at your spiritual disciplines, and "nothing's happening." Maybe you have given lots of time to your disciplines, and it feels as though God has abandoned you, after all. "Why bother?" you may ask.

As a safeguard against relapses, choose to watch over your mental processes with vigilance. Watch your thoughts. Pay attention to your patterns. Memorize Psalm 19:14, and then *live it.*

In the spiritual journey, you can find a rhythm that fits your temperament and your energy level. You can vary your routine so you won't get bored or hypnotize yourself with habit.

If you take a day off from your relationship with God, what happens? Is it worth it?

Psalm 18:1-3

When you have a chronic physical condition, you learn to hear the signals from your body that alert you to the problem before it is full-blown.

When you have an addiction, you learn to H.A.L.T. You ask yourself if you are hungry, angry, lonely, or tired, and you take the appropriate measures to address those issues before you turn to the substance, the activity, or the person that you think will soothe your anxiety and numb your pain.

When you feel a spiritual slip coming on, take action! Call for help. Do what you need to do to stop the downward direction.

In the stillness of today, let the words from today's meditation linger in your mind. Speak them slowly, as if you are savoring them.

Picture God-with-you, Emmanuel, in whatever way you can. Perhaps God is simply loving presence. Perhaps you image God as nurturing, gentle, and warm, like a loving mother. Perhaps your image of God is that of father-protector and father-provider.

Go beyond that image and imagine that love is flowing from your heart toward God. Feel love moving from you toward God in a way that is beyond words.

This is not a rational or logical process. There aren't any results you can plan or program. In fact, it is important to give up your attachments to any kind of outcome or results.

For today, simply be in the presence of God and love God.

Do you dare let the love of God be your refuge and your strength? Do you love God?

Psalm 18:4-6

Some thought processes set you up for a relapse. In recovery programs, it's called "stinkin' thinkin'." Spiritual recovery has some of the same pitfalls as any other kind of recovery, and it is essential to be aware of the kinds of things you say to yourself that can set you on a downward spiral.

This time, God won't hear me.

This time, I've gone too far. This is the worst thing I've ever done, and God has surely lost patience with me.

This time, God is looking the other way. He's taking care of people who need him more than I do. Besides, I may not deserve his care.

In the silence, still your mind. Use a prayer word such as "peace," "come, Holy Spirit," or "Jesus" as your focus. Coordinate it with your breathing and repeat it until you feel your mind calming.

Remember the times God intervened to help you when you could not help yourself.

Recall the times God surprised you with a breakthrough moment of grace or an intervention of love. Remember when God gave you what you needed at the moment of your greatest need.

As you remember, let the prayer word "faithful" be the link between you and God. Remind God and yourself that you are counting on the faithfulness of God in this circumstance.

Go ahead. Dare to gamble on the faithfulness of God. Trust God to act. Believe!

Psalm 18:7-29

As you begin this time of silence, recall the picture of God that you create in your own mind. However you want to facilitate that sense of God's presence, do so. Let it include the reality of God's delight in you (v. 19).

One of the ways to avoid a relapse is to be mindful not only of the infinite resources of God, but also the ways in which you have, in the past, acted with courage and boldness, obedience and trust.

In the silence, remember the times when you have done the right thing. Recall the choices that have empowered you instead of debilitated you. Remember when you told the truth about what you were feeling or what you had done. Let yourself take credit for the acts of mercy you have performed, even if they were on behalf of yourself! Feel the pleasure and delight of God directed toward you when you have acted in life-affirming ways.

Let your mind expand to think about the vastness of the resources available to you from the loving hand of God, who longs to bless you and provide for you. God, wants to "keep your lamp burning," to preserve the essence of your true Self, to fill your heart with the spiritual resources you need to do what you were created to do. God wants to keep you from stumbling into a relapse.

As you wait in the silence, imagine that the God of all resources has come to you and is prepared to give you strength, courage, direction, and guidance. How might God fill your life with what you need to keep facing forward instead of slipping backward?

Do you take the necessary time that you require to keep yourself centered in God?

214

Psalm 18:30-45

What is God's intention toward you?

Do you live with the fear that God is out to get you? Do you function with the crippling God-image that keeps you behind barriers, afraid to risk what you know you can do because you think you don't deserve to succeed or you fear making a mistake?

Regularly and consistently, immerse yourself in the verses for today. Linger over each verse, letting the its implications sink deeply into your mind and heart. Affirm often that God intends to love you and empower you to do what he created you to do.

In the silence, imagine yourself being protected by God. What does that mean to you?

What would be different in your life if you were strengthened by God, whose name is Love? What kind of strength does Perfect Love give? What kind of strength does Perfect Love require? How does a person empowered by Perfect Love treat other people, starting with herself?

Imagine the grace and gracefulness of a human being guided by the hand of God. What would it mean for you to know that your feet and hands were energized and directed by the One who made you?

Knowing you have instant access to the God of all creation has a way of helping you cross that moment when you could choose up or down.

What do you think God wants to give you on this day? Will you accept it?

Psalm 18:46-50

Are you ever reminded of a time when you did everything "right" and still failed?

Are you wallowing in self-pity, recalling the ways you have served God only to keep struggling and fighting to persevere?

Do you think God has favorites, and you aren't one of them? Are you looking for excuses that will justify a relapse into depression, practical atheism, cynicism, skepticism, rage, or self-pity?

Are you afraid to try the high road again after what happened to you last time? Are you more afraid of failure or success? Do you believe God is in the midst of it all, regardless of how you interpret the outcomes?

Failures and detours, disappointments and mistakes are part of being human. In fact, they are almost essential to the maturing process, for the things that don't turn out as we'd like often teach us the most. Stuff happens, even when you do your best.

Ultimately, God and God's ways will triumph, no matter what. Finally and eventually, the will of God will overcome everything else.

In the silence, lift your eyes from your present state or your current circumstances and look far into the horizon. God sees the big picture of your life. Ultimately, God will not fail.

What does that mean for you today? Keep facing forward, and trust.

What is the next thing indicated for you to do? Do it now. Keep moving. Trust in God.

Facing and Feeling Your Fears

Letting the Faith Keep You

On the morning of September 11, 2001, when terrorists forever changed the belief that the American people were invincible, I was leading a contemplative prayer retreat at the Cenacle Retreat Center in Houston, Texas. One of the retreatants came to me at breakfast and whispered to me that disaster had struck. As fate would have it, we were to spend the morning praying Psalm 46.

We went on with our morning's agenda, but in a different mode from the one I had planned. Shocked, stunned, appalled, and introduced to a new kind of fear, we sought refuge and strength in the ancient words of the psalmist who also knew the terrors of the night and the fears of the day.

With only the beginning of an understanding of what it meant for the world to crumble, we turned to the Source of ultimate protection. We knew we would never be the same again.

There are no guarantees for believers or unbelievers against terrorists' attacks or the ravages of disease. Trouble happens, and we all live with an existential angst in a world of violence and danger. Fear is part of the human condition. It is a primitive emotion that every human being experiences at some level.

In the end, we must choose, day by day, to face the fear and then choose the ways of faith and hope and life. We must acknowledge the reality of our fears. It helps to name them, but we must choose to live with courage and boldness in the face of what we fear most.

We return over and over to the affirmations of the psalms. Regardless of the valley of death through which we walk, we can choose courage and love over fear.

Psalm 46:1-3

"I can do whatever I need to do, if I can just push through this terrible fear that cripples me."

"The problem itself isn't insurmountable. *Fear* is the thing that has me paralyzed."

"I can face almost anything, if I know that God is with me."

Fear. Does it make you freeze or flee? Or are you someone who attacks the object of your fear? It is fear, after all, that lurks beneath the surface of arrogance and harshness.

Do you know what you fear? Can you name your fears? Are you aware that beneath afflictive emotions such as jealousy, greed, anger, rage, envy, guilt, shame, and hate, *fear* bubbles like a toxic river, contaminating your inner life?

Over and over, Jesus implored, *"Fear not!"* He said it so many times, in fact, that we are obliged to examine the stand we must take against it.

In the middle of the biggest trauma, if you can go to that quiet center of your innermost being, you will find God. If, in the most terrible crisis, you can somehow make your way to that affirmation of the presence of God who is "refuge and strength, ever-present help in trouble," you will have the resources you need to transcend the crises and to overcome your fears.

Before the crisis or need, however, you can practice the presence of God in daily meditation. Starting now, you can "install" the coping mechanism of faith by positioning God in your own mind and heart. Pray this psalm in the calm times, and it will serve you in the storms.

Hold to this psalm as an anchor. It is timeless, proven, and trustworthy.

Psalm 46:4

DAY TWO

In your imagination, walk down a gently sloping hill to the bank of a quiet river. Feel the sunshine on your back and the breeze on your face. Look above you to a brilliant blue sky. Hear the wind playing through the branches of the trees that line the river. Enjoy the song of a bird perched on a tree across the river. Let the colors of nature come to you, and give thanks that you can see them. After all, God could have made the world in black and white.

As you sit on the grass beside the river, make yourself comfortable. Take deep breaths. Look around you at this sacred sanctuary. Then, focus your attention on the movement of the river. Notice the sun dancing in the water. Hear the sound it makes, traveling toward its destination.

Close your eyes and let the symbol of the river take you to the active presence of God, flowing through all of creation. Let the peacefulness of that movement touch you in the places where you hold fear. Let the waters flow through the places where you have trapped fear in your body, cleansing those wounds and healing your tattered edges. Let fear flow out of you, washed away in the current of the river. Let the assurance of God's presence flow through you like the river flows through the riverbed.

In the silence, let your mind linger on the necessity of water in the natural world. Let your mind return to the necessity of God's presence, flowing through you. Let that presence bring gladness to your inner life.

Let the river of God's love flow through you daily. Make it a habit.

What can you do to remember that the river of God is always with you?

Psalm 46:4-7

Go ahead and *name* your fears. Know what they are. Differentiate between your anxiety, which is free-floating, and your fear, which has an object. Identify the places you fear, the stimuli that provoke your fears, and your current coping mechanisms for controlling your fears. Then ask yourself how well those coping mechanisms work for you.

As you can, go ahead and *feel* your fear. Let the feeling come to you. In fact, *go into the fear. Feel it. Identify where you put it in your body.* You may want to sift and sort through your fears until you identify the various ones that cause you trouble. You may even want to rank them. Know the enemy, and then turn it into a helper.

Now that you are *aware*, you can accept the fear for what it is. You can take responsibility for it. As long as it is hidden from you in the hideout of denial, you can't do anything about it. Brought into the light, you can start working with it.

As you sit in the silence, aware of your fear, *abandon* that fear into the heart of God. Surrender the specific fear to God. Speak your surrender *out loud!*

Nature abhors a vacuum, so ask God to fill the empty space left by fear with love, confidence, and courage.

You have surrendered your fear to God.

In *faith,* begin to behave in a new way, the way of confidence and love.

Keep practicing the new behaviors, and the *feeling* of faith will follow.

Take a stand against fear! You can help keep the river of gladness flowing.

Psalm 46:8-9

DAY FOUR

It's an inside job, this conquering of fear. What happens on the outside of us has to happen first on the inside.

As you enter into the silence today, assess the cost of fear in your life. Take a look at your physical symptoms. Is fear attached to them some way and somehow?

What causes that knot in your stomach? When does that pain in your neck appear? In whose presence does that heavy sensation in your chest show up? What about that fidgety, frantic, frenetic lifestyle you're living? What is that fear about, anyway?

In what ways are you your own worst enemy? How do you wreak havoc in your own life? What are the ways you have brought desolation in your own world? Underneath these presenting problems, there is fear. Wouldn't it be better to find the fear and deal with that instead of continuing to fight the old wars that never end?

Where are you at war with yourself? Is there some part of your life where you feel one way, but behave in another, creating conflicts that you have to palliate with drugs, alcohol, food, or shopping? What hurts and causes you to fight wars on the outside of you? What is the fear underneath it all? And is your biggest fear *knowing* the truth about that thing that hurts?

What bows and spears do you use on yourself and others? Where are you using your wounds as weapons? Wouldn't it be better to face the real enemy, your fear?

In the silence, be willing to tell yourself the truth about what you fear the most. God is with you, even in the fear. The symptom is the wake-up call. Will you hear it?

Psalm 46:10

"You will keep in perfect peace him whose mind is steadfast, because he trusts in you."

—*Isaiah 26:3*

In the uproar of a major crisis or in the panic of an emergency room, the calmest person is the one in charge of the situation and the one who can do the most good.

In the midst of fear, the person who can locate that calm center within himself is the person who can survive the storms of life.

Practicing the spiritual discipline of meditation *before* life falls apart builds strength that will be a resource when the storms come. Practicing meditation, or practicing the presence of God, on a regular basis is the way of accessing the power and peace of God. It is the way of cooperating and collaborating with the intent of God. It is the way of abiding in Christ.

In the silence, breathe deeply and silently repeat the words of the psalm.

Be.

Be still.

Be still and know.

Be still and know that I am God.

Let yourself remember that when you pray these ancient words, you join a magnificent cloud of witnesses to the reality of the presence of God that is with you, around you, above you, beneath you, behind you, and before you.

Most important of all, God is within you. Be still and know that often.

Psalm 46:10

DAY SIX

When you are at the end of your ability to do anything about a circumstance, *be still and know the presence of God.*

When there is nothing else you can do, *be still.* When you have exhausted your personal resources, *be still and know the presence of God.*

When you are frantic to fix what is broken, and when you are tempted to do *something,* even if it is wrong, *be still and know the presence of God.*

When you are so afraid that you cannot think, and when terror has you in its grips, *be still and know the presence of God.*

In the silence, move the focus of your attention from the problem at hand and let your mind expand to think about the grandness of God.

Stop holding your breath. Breathe deeply and keep breathing. Instead of dwelling on what you don't have or your feelings of lack, limitation, or inadequacy, consider the adequacy of God.

When you are afraid, call up the image of the vine and the branches of John 15. Let yourself be attached to the vine, a symbol of God. Be a branch and let the life-giving nourishment of God flow into you as silently and purposefully as the life force of the vine flows into the branches.

In the silence, relax and be still. Practice this enough, and you will go naturally to that place of faith and rest when you are most afraid.

In the silence, let God come to you and be for you all that God longs to be.

What is blocking the flow of God's life into your life? Be still and know what it is.

Psalm 46:10

For I am convinced that neither death nor life, neither angels nor demons, neither the present nor the future, nor any powers, neither height nor depth, nor anything else in all creation, will be able to separate us from the love of God that is in Christ Jesus our Lord.

—Romans 8:38-39

What are you allowing to come between you and the presence of God? To what have you given your power, allowing that thing to be the idol that separates you from the love of God?

Who or what do you allow to sit on the high throne of your inner life, bumping off the One True God from the place that is rightfully his?

Is the god you are allowing to come between you big enough for someone like you, a beloved child of God, created in the image of God?

There is no other god that can ultimately meet the challenge of our deepest fears. There is no idol big enough to assuage our fears and no palliative strong enough to address the deep and pervasive pain of fear. There is no activity strenuous enough and no diversion spectacular enough to drown out the constant sound of fear, humming along beneath the surface of all of us.

Choose fearlessness by choosing the God of Love. Choose courage by choosing the Almighty who holds all things together. Choose live in faith each day by choosing to know Immanuel, God with us.

Where will you place your attention? Will you focus on the things that scare you and stay in the places that frighten you, or will you keep your focus on God?

Psalm 77:1-2

Feeling afraid? Admit it!

Feeling afraid? Feel it!

Feeling ashamed of your feelings? Give thanks, instead, for the awesome capacity to *feel*. Only the dead feel no pain!

Is knowing you can feel the fear small comfort when you are in the grips of a panic attack? What good is it, you ask, to know that it is a good thing to be able to feel when the feelings are so strong that you fear you will drown in them?

Principles about managing fear and other strong emotions are good to know:

- Stoicism is not strength. It is emotional lock-down.
- Suppress fear and anger, and you also suppress joy and love.
- What is buried alive stays alive.
- Leave well enough alone when it is, in fact, well enough.

When you start repressing and suppressing emotion, you don't get to pick and choose which feelings you will allow into consciousness and which ones you will avoid. Holding down the pain means holding off the joy and delight, the love and gladness.

In the silence, feel your fears. Walk into the darkness of them, knowing that God is there, and that it is not dark to him. Let yourself cry out to God for help.

When your soul refuses to be comforted, try crying. Tears are the body's way of praying. God hears the prayers of the heart and he hears our crying. Let yourself cry.

Psalm 77:3-6

DAY TWO

Insomnia: God's night school.

Worries and fears: Things that go bump in the night.

This is the psalm for those terrible night hours when things look so bleak and the night seems endless. It is the psalm for the times when your fears keep you from sleeping or startle you awake in the middle of the night. Pray this psalm and let yourself groan.

As you sit up with yourself in the lonely night school of fear, remember that you do not sit up alone. When you cannot articulate your feelings or your prayers, remember that there is One who can intercede for you. When all you can do is groan and weep and cry out in wordless anguish, remember that there is an Interpreter.

In the same way, the Spirit helps us in our weakness. We do not know what we ought to pray for, but the Spirit himself intercedes for us with groans that words cannot express.

—Romans 8:26

If you need to, let yourself feel all of the regret you need to feel. Let your sorrows pour from you freely. Tell yourself the absolute, unvarnished, unequivocal truth about your situation, your fears, your anxieties, and your terrors. Write them down. Speak them aloud. Groan as much as you need to groan.

And then, after you have groaned, move on. Get up out of the depths and entrust your worries to the God of Infinite Love. Claim the empowering presence of God and move on. Morning will come again.

Because of the Lord's great love we are not consumed, for his compassions never fail. They are new every morning; great is your faithfulness.

—Lamentations 3:23

Psalm 77:7-9

As you move into your meditation time, let yourself relax in the presence of God. Breathe deeply, inhaling and exhaling. Use whatever prayer word or Scripture anchors your mind, stilling it and calming it so that you can think more clearly and feel more deeply.

Remind yourself that God is with you. Remember that there is no place you can go where God is not. And then, let your attention go deep within, to that place of the kingdom of God within you. Rest silently, without word or image, in that still and holy space. That is the Holy of Holies within you, and it is always available for you. In fact, that space goes with you no matter where you go.

In the silence of today, let yourself go beyond your fears about external things to the fear of losing your connection to God. Hear the questions of the psalmist as your own questions. Recognize that being absent from God is truly impossible.

Remind yourself that God cannot be other than God is, and that all of your badness, piled up in a huge pile, is *nothing* compared to God's favor, his unfailing love, his mercy, and his compassion. You cannot do anything bad enough to change the nature and character of God, or God's intent toward you.

The only thing you can do to chase God away is to continue to let your fear be bigger than God is. The only thing you can do to block the flow of God's love toward you is to block the flow of God's love for you.

Do you have a way, a word, a practice, or a discipline that keeps you connected to God?

Psalm 77:10–12

God does not turn his head just when you face your crisis. God Almighty does not go out of business just when you need him most. God does not get too busy for you, nor does God require special sacrifices or rituals to get him to notice how much you need him.

In the silence of today, let your mind rest on the facts of the mighty acts of God in history and in your history. Linger on some magnificent moment in your life when you almost couldn't breathe for the wonder of seeing God's creative activity in some specific way. If nothing else, consider the wonder of your own physical being as one of the mighty acts of God.

Consider the mighty act of God in the cross. Ponder the miracle of transformation, when the human Jesus transcended Golgotha and the tomb. Linger lovingly over the miracle of the Risen Christ, whose life has cascaded down through the centuries and into this present moment with you.

It is not God who abandons us, but we who abandon God in a thousand different ways. It is not God who denies us, but we who deny and betray him, often selling the Living Christ for thirty pieces of silver or less.

In the silence, feel your fear of the absence of God.

Then, confess your fear of the *presence* of God, a presence whose white-hot heat demands nothing less than your mind, your heart, your will—your life.

What is it like for you, living with God?

We want God, and we resist God. We long for God, and we run from God. Why?

Psalm 77:13-15

There is always a nagging little voice that chatters in your head, a critical or threatening voice that leads you straight to fear.

We all carry at least one voice in our heads that ridicules or scorns us. Some folks have an entire committee of self-sabotaging voices that cause them to feel inadequate or inferior. Everyone has the name-calling, spirit-busting, confidence-defeating voice that stirs up trouble and inflicts pain, just when they need confidence and courage the most!

In the silence, recall times when the outer circumstances were not nearly as defeating as the inner voices.

In the silence, imagine yourself standing up to those voices and telling them to *be quiet*. In the stillness of your own heart, stand up to those forces within you and ask them to leave. Before fear sets up headquarters in your heart and mind, take a stand against the fear.

Return to these verses over and over. Memorize them and call them up as an antidote to fear. Let the truth in these words and the Truth of the Living God be bigger in your mind and imagination than the lies that feed your fear and anxiety.

Regardless of your present circumstances, God will ultimately bring you to a place of rest and peace.

In spite the facts, and in spite of life's difficulties, God will bring you, ultimately, to safety.

Will you trust God, no matter how you are feeling or what the external facts are?

Psalm 77:16-18

DAY SIX

Are you waiting on God, wondering why God isn't helping you?

Perhaps God is waiting on you! Perhaps you stand in the way of God's intervention! Could it possibly be that you are, in fact, limiting God by an attitude, a behavior, a habit? Perhaps God is yelling at you, "Help me help you!"

How much is fear the block that prevents God's creative, life-giving energy from having its healing, restoring, transforming way in your inner life and in your outer circumstances?

How much is fear the stone that needs to be rolled away in order for the new life in you to spring forth from one of the many tombs and prisons in which humans find themselves?

In the silence, admit the fear that you cannot chase away, no matter what you do. Confess the fear that has a death grip on you, a fear so strong that none of the coping skills or treatment plans you have devised can address them.

Has your fear become a defense, a mechanism to keep you bound in your own prison? Do you cling to your fear as a flight from freedom? Do you maintain your fear, looking for just cause to keep it to avoid stepping into the largeness of your own life? Do you love your fear more than you love freedom?

In the silence, imagine that God comes to you to take away the fear that won't go away. Will you let God do what God can and will and wants to do to help you?

"Do you want to get well?" Jesus asked the lame man. He asks you the same question.

Psalm 77:19-20

Fear not, for I have redeemed you:
I have summoned you by name; you are mine.
When you pass through the waters,
I will be with you;
and when you pass through the rivers, they will not sweep over you.
When you walk through the fire,
you will not be burned; the flames will not set you ablaze.
—Isaiah 43:1-2

The God of the Scriptures is the God of ultimate things, of ultimate safety and of ultimate resolution.

In the meantime—and the mean times—we sometimes get soaked to the skin and experience smoke damage in the ways of life on this earth. Life is difficult for all.

In the meantime, when we are afraid, we turn to God, the Source of courage and confidence. God is not the line of last defense, but the first place we should go when we are afraid.

As you sit in the silence, know that fear is part of the human predicament. It is appropriate, wise, and smart to be afraid of a snake or a person with a gun pointed at your head. It is appropriate to be cautious around people who would use you or abuse you. It is sensible to be conscious of dangers you can avoid. It is not appropriate to live a lifestyle of fear. Or, perhaps, fear is a *deathstyle*.

In the midst of your fears, face forward. Keep moving. Trust God. Choose life!

Psalm 121:1

In fear and despair, the shoulders droop and the human being looks down. The mouth turns downward, and the spirits fall. The psalmist implores, "Look up! Straighten your shoulders. Stand up straight! Lift your focus off your problem and onto the Source of infinite resources, solutions, possibilities, and hope!"

In your mind's eye, create a picture of nature's beauty. Fix in your mind a scene that includes a gently rolling hilltop or, if you choose, a mountain peak. Color it in all of the splendors of nature. See the clear, blue sky behind it. Breathe in, and imagine that you are filling your lungs with pure and clean mountain air. Inhale and know that you breathe in the very breath of God.

As you hold this mental picture in your mind, let the higher elevations lift your thoughts beyond even the beauty of the creation to the Creator. Hold that thought—the thought of the grandness and magnificence of God—in your mind.

When your mind wants to wander back to that thing you use to scare yourself, don't fight that thought or the fear. Simply acknowledge it. Tell it you know it is there, but for this season of time, you are going to focus on something bigger than your greatest fear.

Don't try to address the problem of your fear. Don't try to solve the problem that causes your fear. In fact, don't do anything except hold the grandeur of the mountain scene and the magnificence of God in your attention.

As you sit in the silence, keep returning to the reality of the presence of God.

Lift your attention to higher things. Lift your focus to God. Lift your fear to God.

Psalm 121:1

DAY TWO

How easy it is to let ourselves go astray and wander into the wasteland of fear and despair! What a temptation it is to go our own way and wind up in the fields where the landmines of worry, terror, and anxiety wait for us!

When fear sets in, or when you feel it coming on, acknowledge it. Call it what it is, and then choose to train your focus on something really big. When you are afraid, instead of letting your heart, mind, and soul shrivel up in a huddle, chanting "what if's," turn your attention toward the timeless, the trustworthy, and the true.

Instead of wringing your hands in frustration before what you cannot change, train yourself to sit down, turning your palms up in a gesture of trust and openness to the vast resources of an infinite Creator.

In the silence, bring your attention to your hands. Place them in your lap, palms up and open. Breathe deeply, soothing yourself with each breath.

Bring your mind home from its wanderings in fields of fear and let it rest on the timeless, silent majesty of God. Let the mental image of the mountain symbolize for you the strength and magnificent presence of God.

Hold that image for as long as you need to, letting your breath go deeper and deeper. Be willing to rest in God's presence, trusting that God is holding you and all that concerns you in the palm of his hand. Let your open hands remind you of God's hands.

Does the image of the mountain lift your heart to God? If not, what does?

Psalm 121:1

DAY THREE

Can a mother forget the baby at her breast,
and have no compassion on the child she has borne?
Though she may forget, I will not forget you!
See, I have engraved you on the palms of my hand.

—*Isaiah 49:15-16*

From where does your true and ultimate help come, except from God?

To be sure, a friend or a priest, a soulmate or a counselor is "God with skin on" at various times in your life, but at the end of the day, it's your lonesome valley to walk with your fear. In the end, each of us must wrestle with our own fears in the interior landscape of our lives.

You can soothe yourself. You can numb and distract yourself. You can come up with elaborate treatment programs to manage your fear, but until you can find the wellspring of power, presence, and love from within, you will forever be dependent on external helpers.

Typically, all that is external to you works only for a while. Usually, all other sources of comfort finally fail. Only God and the timeless Truth of God's presence ultimately addresses the fears that lurk and linger in the human heart.

Return as many times as necessary during the day to the image of the hilltop, lifting your mind and attention away from the problem at hand to the grandeur of God.

Rest in the assurance that God will not leave you and that God is with you always, in all places.

What is your personal plan for holding the awareness of God in your mind?

Psalm 121:2

Before they call, I will answer;
while they are still speaking, I will hear.

—Isaiah 65:24

Imagine the magnificence of this: The creator of the heavens and the earth, the Transcendent God, is lovingly attentive to the call of his children.

Think about the wonder of this: The Maker of the mountains and hills draws near to respond to the voice of his children.

The initiative is always from God to you. The very thought to turn toward God in prayer is a sign that the Loving God has tapped you on the shoulder and wants to start a conversation with you. Prayer is the means through which God speaks to you; God is always praying to you.

In the silence, let your mind be still and quiet in the presence of God. Be assured that God speaks to you.

In the silence, be willing to hear the voice of God. It may come through an intuitive hunch, an inner nudging, an insight, a revelation. You will know it is God if it carries the energy and power of love and peace. Even if what God says is hard for you to hear, you will, with patient practice, come to know the sound of God's voice, just as the sheep knows the sound of the shepherd's voice.

God's voice brings wisdom, comfort, and guidance. God's voice is the voice of liberty and liberation. God's voice extends forgiveness and mercy. God's voice is truly *helpful*.

You may have to ask other voices to be quiet so that you can hear the voice of God.

Psalm 121:3-4

I will lead the blind by ways they have not known,
along unfamiliar paths I will guide them;
I will turn the darkness into light before them,
and make the rough places smooth.
These are the things I will do;
I will not forsake them.

—*Isaiah 42:16*

When you are afraid, return to this psalm and to the words of the prophet Isaiah. Linger over them until the Spirit of God kneads their truth down deep into your heart.

God is on-call, twenty four hours a day.

God never goes off-duty.

God is constant.

God will guide you, watch over you, and protect you.

If you are afraid, affirm that God's perspective is the perspective of your whole life, played against the backdrop of all of history. God is alive, active, and dynamic in the midst of your life.

If you are stumbling, call for help! If you are going over an edge and into the abyss, call for help! If you are terrified, call for help!

In the still place within your heart, center yourself by focusing on the presence of God. However hard the road is for you at this point, count on the ultimate plan of God. If all seems lost, count on the ultimate plan of God. If you are afraid, rest in God.

If you cannot see the hand of God, trust the heart of God. Trust and obey.

Psalm 121:5-6

Though the mountains be shaken and the hills be removed,
yet my unfailing love for you will not be shaken . . . .

—Isaiah 54:10

Bad things happen to good people.

Harder still to reconcile is the reality that good things happen to bad people.

Within the secret recesses of the human heart, in that inner prayer closet, the work of faith goes on. It is within that inner kingdom that God does his best work, strengthening the ties that bind the human heart to the heart of the Divine. It is there, on the inside, that fear is conquered and love and power are installed.

In the silence, ask God to move deep within that secret place and do whatever he needs to do to establish his spirit within you. Give the Divine Therapist permission to move deeply within your old thought patterns and habitual responses to address the emotional programming of a lifetime, programming that leads you to a place of fear instead of love. Ask God to replace all impulses of inappropriate fear with his resources.

Make a plan of discipline to help God do what God wants to do. Let the disciplines of consistent prayer and meditation lead you to inner health and wholeness.

For God did not give us a spirit of timidity, but a spirit of power, of love
and of self-discipline.

—2 Timothy 1:2

Does your fear really get you where you want to go? Does your anxiety
and worry?

Psalm 121:5-6

. . . for I am with you to rescue and save you. I will save you from the hands of the wicked, and redeem you from the grasp of the cruel.
—Jeremiah 15:20b-21

Look around you and you will find all kinds of evidence that argues with the promises expressed in the Psalms and in Jeremiah.

Read the newspaper and watch the evening news and collect data to support your clinging to your fears.

Check out your own history, if you've lived long enough, and remember, if you can bear it, the names of the people who have hurt you. Few people escape the arrows of the wicked and the cruel; no one is immune to the inadvertent, accidental, and unintentional woundings within the life of the family and the families of faith.

In the silence of today, lift your eyes from the behavior of fallible and finite, flawed and frail human beings. Take your attention off the various offenses inflicted on you. For the moment, move your focus off that festering wound of another's rejection or abandonment. Remove your gaze from your favorite fear.

Today, reaffirm the intention of God toward you and toward all human creatures, and remember how hard God has to work to do his mighty and tender acts of loving-kindness through the barriers and blocks of human pride and arrogance, willfulness, and selfishness. Consider what an incredible thing it is for God to reach us at all, given all he must work through and around, in the course of a day!

Are you placing anything between you and God? How hard do you make God work?

Psalm 121:7-8

Behold . . . I am doing a new thing . . . I am making a way in the desert, and streams in the wasteland.

—*Isaiah 43:18*

For my thoughts are not your thoughts,
neither are your ways my ways, declares the LORD.

—*Isaiah 55:8*

Just because you cannot see what God is doing, it doesn't mean that nothing is happening!

Just because you don't recognize the new path in the desert doesn't mean that it isn't there!

You may be standing at the window, frantically searching for the appearance of God in some form you can recognize or in some pattern he used last year, when he is standing at the door of your heart, knocking persistently and lovingly.

After all, God wants to dwell in the heart. While God is alive in every part of creation, the reality is that God's geography is not so much of the land as it is the human heart.

As you learn to live with fear, counteract its toxic effects by immersing yourself in the Scriptures. Take the written words to heart, memorizing them and meditating on them, and let them lead you over and over to the Living Word, the Spirit of God who broadcasts love. Let the written word light your path to the Light of the world.

Your word is a lamp to my feet and a light to my path.

—*Psalm 119:105*

What is your line of defense against the ordinary fears of everyday life and the extraordinary terrors of the catastrophic and the terrible?

I Believe: Trust and Obey

How hard it is to place trust in a being you cannot see or touch! What a stretch it is to obey an invisible force! No wonder we humans place our trust in objects that we can manipulate and control, measure and contain. Who wouldn't project the inward need for a god onto a human person such as a pastor, a priest, a teacher, a parent, or a spouse? And when those lesser gods fail us, how logical it is to decide that God does not exist or that God cannot be trusted.

It is natural for human beings to devise elaborate systems of theology and doctrine to try to grasp the ineffable, mysterious, transcendent God. And when life does not fit into our neat systems, we naturally give up on God.

The need for God is inborn, written into the very heart of the human person, and the need to be connected to God is as natural as the need to survive and thrive. Praying the psalms nurtures what is natural.

Regular, consistent, and conscious affirmation of God—the God of the psalmist—has an amazing and mysterious power to deepen the capacity to trust in the One who is ultimately trustworthy. The language of the psalms lifts the hearts and minds of individuals, transforming the focus of the mind and the thought patterns. Somehow, the feelings follow, spirits are elevated, and change happens within the heart of the pray-er.

Focusing on the God revealed in the psalms somehow increases trust and makes it easier to discern and recognize the guidance of God. True adoration and worship of God facilitate the hard work of obedience. Somehow, it's all connected.

Psalm 101:1

DAY ONE

In the silence of today, make a decision to open your mind and heart to a deeper understanding of your life with God.

Wrap your mind around the idea of trusting and obeying, believing and receiving. Open your mind to seeing the ways in which what you think and do move in harmony with each other. Think about a time in your life when you felt at one with yourself. Think about when you are at odds with yourself, conflicted and locked in an internal battle, not knowing whether to trust your mind or your heart.

In the stillness, let the words of this verse linger in your consciousness. Think what that song of love and justice, coming from your unique life, would be. Would it be filled with harmony, or is it a song of dissonance, so that what you do is at odds with what you think and feel?

Let "singing" be a metaphor of your life with God. Let the idea play in your mind that the melody and the words of a song have integrity. They fit together naturally, each enhancing the other, just as trusting and obeying flow naturally from a heart in alignment with the heart of God.

You can choose how your life with God will be. It can be a war hymn and a battle cry, all the way to the end. It can be a funeral dirge or a lament. You get to choose. However you decide your life with God will be, that is how it will be. It's up to you.

What would it take for your life with God to be a hymn of praise or a love song?

Psalm 101:2

Your life with God does not have to be left to chance. You are not at the mercy of your pastor or faith community. You are not a passive object, doomed to wait until the right spiritual leader comes along to show you the way to God!

Neither is life with God about staying childish and being nagged by a punitive parent. God wants to bring forth the best in you! He isn't about forcing you to do what you hate to do. Life with God isn't about holding your nose while you take bad medicine. It isn't about slogging through life, grimly doing your duty.

It's up to you, basically. You get to choose the quality of your life with God. God pours out love, guidance, and resources for the person who chooses to see. God desires intimacy with you, but you have to choose what God holds out to you.

In the silence, become aware of residual, childish belief that tells you life with God is about following rules and checking off squares in a six-point record system. Move your focus to a broader perspective, a more adult view, and open your mind to the idea that the "blameless" way is the way of intimacy with God.

It is as if God invites you to dance with him in an incredibly beautiful dance designed just for you, to show your strengths and abilities in their best light. And you dance to the most beautiful music imaginable.

The task, then, for every *follower* is to let God lead. The challenge in the dance is to trust the One who leads! Life with God is about cooperating and collaborating with the One who knows the music and the steps and who does all things well.

It's your responsibility. Keep dancing solo, or choose to dance with God.

Psalm 101:3

Finally . . . whatever is true, whatever is noble, whatever is right, whatever is pure, whatever is lovely, whatever is admirable—if anything is excellent or praiseworthy—think about such things.

—Philippians 4:8

Whatever you think about, you bring about.

Harbor a thought. The behavior follows.

Repeat the behavior. Habits form.

How you think about God, over time, determines how freely you are able to let go and trust God. How you feel about God determines how willingly or joyfully you obey God.

As you reflect on your life with God today, scan your thought patterns. Do the things that occupy your mind give you energy? Are your thoughts life-giving and life-affirming? Or is your mind consumed with worry and resentment?

Do you focus on the gifts of God, lavished on creation, or do you tend to look for the war stories, the conflicts, the evidence of human depravity? Do you look for evidence to prove that God is trustworthy, or do you keep God locked in a box of distrust?

Do you take time to appreciate what God has already given you, or are you focused on what you don't have?

It's a powerful instrument, that mind of yours, and whatever you allow to reside in it affects every part of your life.

You are the custodian of your mind. You are a steward of your gifts.

Does your thought life lead you to deeper trust and greater obedience or away from them?

Psalm 101:4-5

DAY FOUR

There is a cast of characters in your outer world, and there is another cast of characters within your inner world. How well do those in both worlds support your life with God? Our mothers are right: we are known—and shaped—by our friends.

Take time to observe the various characters that populate your outer world. You received some by chance or by mindless choice. Others you drew to you, and still others chose, deliberately and consciously.

With what kinds of people do you spend your life, day after day? Are they people who support a life of integrity? Do they encourage you in your faith life? Are you enlarged or diminished by the people with whom you work and play? Do they make it easy or hard for you to live in belief, trust, and obedience?

Moving your focus to that inner cast of characters, remind yourself that your name is Legion. There are many voices within you—some that encourage and support your life with God, and others that cast doubt and skepticism into your heart.

Which is the strongest voice within you? Is it the voice of the Living God, calling you to a life of integrity, truth, authenticity, meaning, and purpose? Or is the loudest voice the voice that lies to you about who you are and who God is?

Becoming aware and conscious of that committee inside your head and the people in your outer life helps you make choices that ease your trust and obedience of the Living God, who speaks within the sanctuary of the human heart.

Whose voice would you most like to hear calling the shots in your inner life?

Psalm 101:6

"Stick with the winners. The losers will get you drunk."
—*traditional Alcoholics Anonymous advice*

Somewhere in the life of the serious seeker after God, there has to be a circle of friends and fellow seekers seriously devoted to God.

Somewhere in the course of a seven-day week, there has to be a sacred space in which people attempting the journey of life in faith and attempting to trust and obey the dynamic call of God can meet together and encourage each other.

Somewhere, deep within the recesses of your own heart, there has to be a connection with the Living God, a connection that will not fail you when the outer voices demand your conformity to culture, urging you to take the easy way out, to go for the quick fix and the instant solution.

Both the outer circle of faithful friends and the inner voice of God are necessary for the bold and daring lifestyle that requires radical trust and radical obedience.

Take a look at your life. Where are you getting your deep soul needs met? Who are the faithful that will not let you deviate off the path of wholeness? Who are the people who can see into your soul and will not let you take the low road?

What do you do to cultivate the connection with that inner voice of God, who is always faithful? Are you as faithful to that voice as that voice is to you?

How are you keeping your soul supported on the Way?

It's your responsibility and your choice to find the support you need for your faith life.

Psalm 101:7

Make a decision to live a life of radical truth and see what happens.

Make a decision to root out the lies in your belief system, and watch your life change.

Make a decision to give up pretending that something isn't what it really is. Choose to give up denial forever. Give up going along with a group lie just so somebody in the group will not feel uncomfortable. Refuse to collude with a system built on any kind of lie.

Before you do that, however, you'd better buckle your seatbelt, because the ride of truth-seeking and truth-knowing and truth-telling is bumpy! This is the psalm of radical change, and the change begins within your own inner life. This is the verse that should carry a sign that says, WARNING! DANGER AHEAD.

It's not the people *out there* that you should think about, but those voices within you that keep you from knowing the truth and speaking the truth *to yourself and to God!*

There is a Voice of Truth within you. It may be buried under layers of pretense and denial, half-truths and little white lies, but it is there, waiting for you to excavate it so your soul can be set free.

There is, within you, the Voice of Truth that knows what you are to do, if you are willing to turn to that Voice, honor it, and listen to it. It is your sacred responsibility and your moral obligation to hear that Voice. It is a gift you can give your world.

Go ahead. Start with that thing you've been wanting to hide. You know what it is.

Psalm 101:8

DAY SEVEN

"Do you mean I have to do this every day?" the brand new arrival to the recovery group asked his sponsor. "I can't just get it all at once?"

"You aren't able to take it in all at once, kid. You've got to get it one morsel at a time, just like everyone else. You aren't special. You aren't different. You don't get to create a new set of rules that have worked for thousands of recovering people, over long years of trial and error."

One day at a time. For everyone.

Every day, you get to start over. Yes—you, too.

Sometimes, you have to start your day again an hour after you started the first time. That's just the way it is.

Eternal vigilance is, after all, the price of freedom, and there is no one—*no one*—immune to the perils of slipping away from the daily disciplines of following God.

A lifetime of living in willfulness and independence isn't changed overnight. The light on the Damascus road may have blinded Saul and brought him to his knees, but it took some years before Saul became Paul.

In the silence, give thanks that the mercies of God are new and available for you every morning. God is the Source of life and love and liberty, and from God you receive what you need to keep facing forward, trusting and obeying.

Make a choice, starting now, to keep showing up for that appointment with God. Make a choice to let your life be a song sung in harmony with the music of God.

Psalm 103:1

DAY ONE

I will sing of the LORD'S great love forever;
with my mouth I will make your faithfulness known
through all generations.
I will declare that your love stands firm forever,
that you established your faithfulness in heaven itself.

—*Psalm 89:1-2*

When you cannot decide whether to trust God and obey what you believe is God's guidance, spend time in this psalm.

When you are confused, torn between two paths, take your mind off the decision-making process and return to this psalm. When you are conflicted, caught in ambivalence, ambiguity, or anxiety, let this psalm refocus your attention on the present help who is God. Reflect on the words of this psalm. Bring the doubting, warring parts of your entire inner committee into the silence, and rest in the presence of a holy God.

When it appears that God asks what is too hard for you, wait. Redirect your attention away from what is too hard for you and toward the One for whom nothing is too hard.

When you are burned out and have given everything, let this psalm be the focus of your meditation, and begin by simply affirming (praising) God for who God is. If you can't get to that place, simply sit with your willingness to affirm God. If you can't get there, take a nap! When you are exhausted, taking a nap is the most spiritual thing you can do.

Take time to measure your spiritual temperature before you take any action.

Psalm 103:2-3

But those who hope in the LORD
will renew their strength.
They will soar on wings like eagles;
they will run and not grow weary,
they will walk and not be faint.

—*Isaiah 40:31*

Renewal. Re-creation. Restoration. Resurrection.

What serious seeker after God doesn't, at some point along the way, need a resting place for renewal and restoration?

Oh, that I had in the desert
a lodging place for travelers,
so that I might leave my people
and go away from them . . .

—*Jeremiah 9:2*

It is impossible—completely impossible—to stay on the spiritual path of life in a materialistic world without regular and consistent resting, resting for the purpose of re-creation. How can you know what to do with and for God if you don't *know* God?

It is impossible to discern the direction and guidance of God without taking advantage of time alone with God. However, the time apart is not the "time-out" for misbehavior in the corner of the schoolroom. The time apart is for the purpose of tapping into the vast resources of God, for being forgiven and healed, for experiencing firsthand the love and compassion of God.

When was the last time you drew apart to be renewed through intimacy with God?

Psalm 103:5

DAY THREE

"I am making everything new!"

—Revelation 21:5

There's a funny thing about life with God. You can't really know how utterly trustworthy God is until you take the leap to trust him.

There's another funny thing about life with God. Belief isn't intellectual assent as much as stepping into the unknown, where the Known always waits. Somehow, God waits to see if you open your mind and heart to the possibilities he has in store for you, and then he moves to give you what you need.

In the silence, bring your weary self to God. Bring that part of you that is worn-out from doing good. Bring that part of you that is starved for nourishment, and bring that part of you that is sick and afflicted. Bring even that part of you that is sick and tired of being sick and tired.

Bring that part of you that wants to trust and obey. Bring that part of you that is needy and afraid. Bring that part of yourself that longs to be renewed, the part that feels dead.

In the stillness, just wait. You don't have to figure out how God is going to renew you. You don't have to come up with his plan for him. You don't even have to decide if he wants to renew you or if you have earned the blessings of rejuvenation.

All you have to do is show up and lay your emptiness before the One who desires good things for you and whose very nature is to make all things new.

Does your God-concept include this re-creating aspect of the Creator? Is this for you?

Psalm 103:6-12

"You need to fire that god and get a God who loves you!"
—spiritual director to a directee

In sickness and hard times, the real God-concept shows up! When crisis hits, that God-concept you carry at an emotional level, and not the one you proclaim in Sunday school or church, is the one that appears.

In trouble, you get to challenge the worn-out concepts of God that no longer work for you. If the concept of God you carry at an emotional, irrational, and unconscious level is a punishing, spiteful deity, stand up to that concept and banish it from your inner kingdom, for it has nothing to do with the God of Love. You aren't going to want to follow any other god than the God the psalmist describes in this passage!

Take each verse of this passage and ask yourself some hard questions.

Do I think God is accusing me and holds a grudge forever?

Do I live as if God's love is limited?

Do I live as if I am on parole or as if I am an unwanted child?

In the stillness of today and in the holiness of this time, choose to place your trust in the God of compassion and mercy. Choose to change your mind, if you need to, and let God be the one whose compassions never end.

Isn't that the God you can trust? Isn't that the God you are able and willing to follow and obey? It is this God who beckons you to come home to his heart.

When was the last time you felt the compassion of God toward you? That's too long.

Psalm 103:13-16

How wonderful it is to be known for who you are!

Is there anything more freeing than being with someone who accepts you for who you are, no matter how you may be?

How freeing it is to be in the presence of someone who allows you to be all of who you are, who understands your idiosyncrasies and faults, your biases and blind spots, and loves you in spite of them!

In the silence, remember the God of Psalm 139. That's the God who made you and watches over you. That's the God the psalmist knew, the one who understands that we humans are all basically pretty good people, yet flawed and imperfect. God understands that we stumble and fall and that we need countless chances to begin again.

Do you know where the fault lines of your own soul are? Are you aware of the places that trap and trick you? Can you give the same compassion to yourself that God does? If not, why not?

Linger with this God who understands. Allow this God who surrounds you with loving-kindness, grace, and mercy to move toward you and fill those broken places in your heart and mind with the balm of his presence.

Could it be that the greatest challenge in your life is trusting God enough to accept his opinion of you? Could the obedience God asks of you be the obedience of accepting his loving-kindness for you?

Does your concept of God keep you bound in misery, or does it set you free for joy?

Psalm 103:16-18

DAY SIX

"I cannot tell you what to do. This is your decision. What I can tell you is this: If you make the right decision, and things turn out well for you, that is good. But if you make the wrong decision, you will learn important lessons that, perhaps, you needed to learn. And that, too, is good."
—from a very wise parent to her child

Make the wrong decision, and God is there.

That is what the psalmist says. God's everlasting love is everywhere, even to the ends of the earth.

Make the right decision, and God is there, too.

Make sure you don't forget him in the good times.

Today, as you reflect on the everlasting love of God, let that love lead you to reverence of God.

As you bring to your mind the decisions you must make, keep your connection to the God whose love is everlasting.

In your mind's eye, conceptualize the decision you must make as an actual object that you can hold in your hands. See yourself sitting with this object in the presence of God. Wait and see what God has to say about that decision.

Are you willing to follow the direction God gives you? Does that direction feel life-affirming or life-depleting? God is on the side of life!

Perhaps the first choice to make in the face of any hard decision is to love God.

Psalm 103:20-22

"God is Spirit, and his worshipers must worship in spirit and in truth."
—*John 4:24*

Perhaps it can be said that spirituality is about our life with God, and the truth is that we cannot not be spiritual beings. Perhaps it is also true that religion is about our external practices that enhance—or diminish—our life with God.

In the holy space within, that space where you and God are alone, let your mind linger on the reality of the Love of God. The inner work of intimacy with God is necessary for radical trust and obedience.

The God revealed in this psalm is the One who beckons you into a life of wholeness. This is the One who cares about your happiness and welfare, and more importantly, the One who cares about your *wholeness.*

Whatever God asks of you is intended to bring you toward wholeness. It is not the perfection of looking good externally. It is not about image or perception, but about the nature of your inner life. And sometimes that way seems treacherous and dangerous.

Whatever God asks of you, however hard it is, God will provide the ways and the means to get you where he wants you to go.

Whatever God starts in you, God wants to finish. Therefore, trust God . . . and act boldly. God is with you!

Somewhere, you know what God is asking of you. You keep bringing your requests to him, but have you taken time to hear his requests of you?

God wants to make you whole! Do you trust him enough to let him do that?

Psalm 145:1-7

Pray this psalm when you are paralyzed and frozen, unable to move because of the death wrappings of *performance anxiety.*

The fear of failure. The fear of trying. The fear of rejection and ridicule.

The memory of all the times you failed in the past. The shudder that comes with the memory of shameful defeat. The fear of humiliation.

The fear of not being enough. The fear of doing the wrong thing.

The fear of success. Procrastination. The crippling paralysis of trying to be perfect. The fear of being wrong. The fear of making a fool of yourself.

In the silence, name what cripples your *belief,* that active response to the initiative of God. Be specific. Know what stimulates that fear response. Become aware of how you keep yourself stuck, trapped in a belief system at odds with the dynamic, active, life-giving, love-lavishing energy of God that wants you to step forward into a wider place of freedom.

In the silence, hear the voice of God calling your name, beckoning to you to join him in a venture of grace. Trust isn't about you. It's about God!

In the silence, let your fears sit aside in your mind, and bring to center stage the image of God that the psalmist defines.

To follow, you must give up your fear of making a mistake. To obey God, you must get over your need to *do it right.* Just go where God leads, and see what happens! Give God a chance to heal your fear of performance, all the way down to its origin.

Do you dare step out of the past and into the largeness of your own life with God?

Psalm 145:8-13

DAY TWO

What power there is in the words we speak! How amazing are the thoughts we think, over and over.

It's almost as if God is as big for us as we allow him to be. It's almost as if when we believe God is not adequate, he isn't, and when we take the chains off God and accept that there is no end to his resources or his Love, that becomes true for us.

In the silence, ponder the words of the psalmist. Where do you find it hard to allow the grandeur of God to be true in your own life? Where does the bigness of God want to be set free in your life? How are you holding God hostage, making him conform to a limited and limiting space that isn't nearly big enough for God?

As you rest in the presence of God, speak each verse of this passage aloud. Slowly coordinate your breathing with each verse.

As you exhale, breathe out all limited and limiting beliefs that you hold about God, and with those beliefs, the accompanying fears.

As you inhale, breathe in the words of this mighty psalm. Let the omnipotence of God be the measure of your expectation. Let God be as big as God longs to be!

Notice, as you wait in the silence, where your resistance is. Where do your doubts rise, taunting you to diminish God? About what issues in your life do you most habitually limit God? How do you hold God in the docks, demanding that he behave as some human deity you worship behaves?

Breathe even more deeply. Give God room to work in your mind and heart.

If you believe something is true, it will be, at least for you. Trust the God who is.

Psalm 145:14-16

So you jumped out there, thinking you were trusting God and obeying him, and you failed.

How do you think Peter felt after he denied Jesus, not once, but three times?

So you risked a lot for the sake of God. You even got out there, in front of everyone, and risked boldly. You risked your reputation and your place in your family, and things didn't work out like you had hoped!

How do you think Mary felt, kneeling at the foot of a criminal's cross, watching her son die?

You launched out into the deep for God, making bold steps on behalf of God. You burned your bridges and poured your life into a new creation, and it seems for all the world that the project is a failure.

How do you think Jesus felt, wrestling with God in Gethsemane?

So, God created human beings with the capacity to choose life or death, blessing or curse. God crowned those humans with such dignity that they were given the choice to be with God or to forsake God.

How do you think God feels, observing his children, some who love him and some who reject him?

How do you think God feels toward you, his beloved creation?

In the silence, put your choices in perspective. Remember that things are not always as they seem. Examine your own heart. If you've failed, get up and go again.

Your failure does not change the nature of God. His love never fails. Count on it.

Psalm 145:17

For it is God who works in you to will and to act according to his good purpose.

—Philippians 2:13

And my God will meet all your needs according to his glorious riches in Christ Jesus.

—Philippians 4:19

It is easy to collect evidence that argues with the words of the psalmist and the words of Paul, but is that really what you want to do when you are gathering your strength to trust and obey the guidance of God?

Of course, you can come up with a list of the times when God doesn't seem to be working in a loving manner toward a portion of his creation! You can sit in the seat of the great high priests of realism and pronounce your cynicism and skepticism from now on, reciting evidence of the times when God doesn't seem to meet the needs of someone!

Does that really serve you?

The invisible God often works in ways that humans cannot see or understand. Sometimes, the spiritual eyes of human beings are so blind or myopic that God can be fast at work in the creation of their lives, and they miss what God is doing.

We miss God because we hold him in the past, expecting him to act in the ways of the past. We lock God up in a variety of ways, but mostly, we lock him up because of our own fear.

In the silence, dare to affirm that in spite of what humans do and how humans respond to the Almighty, you will choose to believe in his unfailing love toward you.

It's a stretch, sometimes, believing in the love of God. Is it worth believing?

Psalm 145:18

Seek the LORD while he may be found;
call on him while he is near.

—Isaiah 55:6

Perhaps you are waiting for God to show up in some cathedral or church before you will venture out and do what he calls you to do. Maybe you want to hear his beckoning from some human instrument on whom you project your own authority. Maybe you think you need proof that God really is out there before you take that step into the unknown.

God often shows up in the oddest places!

God is often in the middle of the darkest shadow in your heart, waiting for you to bring that part of you into the Light.

God is often in the middle of the big problem you don't want to face, beckoning you into it so he can build your strength and your faith muscles.

God is often waiting in the pain that won't go away, wooing you to stop denying how badly it hurts. Sometimes he wants you to trust him enough to go into the pain so he can heal the pain.

God is often hiding in the character defect or addiction you will not admit, calling to you as he called to the dead Lazarus. "Come forth!" he calls.

In the silence, go into the place where you don't want to go. God goes with you. He is near. Trust him, for in God is everlasting life.

Go ahead. What are you waiting for—for it to get worse? God is near. Trust him.

Psalm 145:19-20

Unless the LORD builds the house,
its builder labors in vain.

—Psalm 127:1

In the silence of this day, let your mind wander to the place where you hold your heart's desire. What thing have you always wanted to do? What project is so big that it has to be of God, for it will require the power and resources of God to complete?

What are your unfulfilled longings, those yearnings that you have put in cold storage for any number of reasons?

Without what will your life be incomplete?

To what joint venture is God calling you, a venture that perfectly connects your natural abilities and strengths, your gifts and your interests, with the infinite resources of the Creator of the cosmos?

In the silence, reconnect with that deep desire. Hear your excuses and your reasons for not trusting God and venturing into the unknown. Hear the voices of reason. Pay attention to them, but don't let them be the final authority on what you do.

As you wait with God, wonder what it might mean for God to want to partner with you in a collaborative effort for him. Most likely, what will bring your greatest joy will also please God and serve his children.

What will you do? Will you trust God and help him do what he's called you to do? What will it cost not to follow God where God wants you to go?

Psalm 145:20-21

To him who is able to keep you from falling and to present you before his glorious presence without fault, and with great joy—to the only God our Savior be glory, majesty, power and authority, through Jesus Christ our Lord, before all ages, now and forevermore! Amen.

—Jude 24-25

If you want to question someone, question yourself. Go ahead and be realistic about your resources and limitations. It doesn't hurt to know where your Achilles' heel is. It's smart to know your weaknesses and it's wise to count the risks.

However, the object of your trust is not your own resources. You aren't asked to hope in your own abilities.

As you enter into the silence of this day, place your focus on the Absolute Adequacy of God. Place your trust in God.

Give up your attachment to your own outcomes. Surrender your ideas of how things will work out or whether or not they will work out.

Trusting and obeying God is about ultimate things lived out in the particular details, day by day.

The God of Creation is concerned with the big picture, and you are asked to walk step by step into that big picture.

Take a deep breath. God works *for* you and *with* you and *in* you and *through* you, if you allow him. God accomplishes his purposes, one way or another.

Trust and obey. Trust and obey. Day after day. Trust and obey. There is no other way.

Resting in the Heart of God

"Father, make them one, even as we are one."

—*John 17:11*

"I look at the One who is looking at me."

"I rest in the heart of God, who is in my heart."

The way of peace seems to be resting in God, and that resting seems to be not sleeping or unconsciousness, but a consciousness that regardless of what happens in the outer world, the inner connection between Creator and creature is secure.

The psalmist seemed to live in this state of ongoing communion with God. Even the cry of absence was evidence of the presence of the One who draws near. Even in the midst of the greatest difficulties, the psalmist seemed to experience an intimacy with God that gave him the faith echoed in the words of Julian of Norwich: "All is well; and all shall be well; and all manner of things will be well."

That kind of intimacy is available to those who take the time to cultivate the discipline of practicing the presence of God in the midst of everyday, ordinary life. That deep, inner friendship with God is possible for those willing to enter into that kind of friendship.

God is present everywhere! And life seems, somehow, to be filled with so much more meaning, purpose, and joy for the one who is willing to cultivate the inner eye of seeing and the inner ear of hearing. And the place God wants to live is in the human heart.

"Here I am! I stand at the door and knock. If anyone hears my voice and opens the door, I will come in and eat with him, and he with me."

—*Revelation 3:20*

Psalm 42:1-2

"Blessed are those who hunger and thirst after righteousness, for they will be filled."

—*Matthew 5:6*

"Whoever is thirsty, let him come; and whoever wishes, let him take the free gift of the water of life!"

—*Revelation 22:17*

We are made to hunger and thirst for God. The yearning toward God is at the core of who we are. That hunger and thirst are there for a reason, and the reason is that our hungering and thirsting drive us toward God!

If hunger and thirst are part of us, as creatures made in the image of God, can we also assume that God's plan includes a way for that deep need to be met? Of course!

There are certain churches in which the communion bread and cup are brought to the congregants, just as God sometimes brings gifts to us.

In other churches, believers get up from their pews and walk to the altar to receive the communion elements. Sometimes, God wants us to get up off our resting places and go get what he has for us!

Both methods have value, and each teaches something different about the activity of God.

In the silence of today, get in touch with your hunger and thirst for God. Let it become big in your inner experience.

If you do not have that kind of longing for God, ask God for the longing.

You are intended to want to be with God. If you don't, are you numbing that thirst?

Psalm 42:3-4

For today, imagine that the psalmist has joined you in the holy space where only you and God reside. Picture him with you, relaxed and in a conversational mood. Hear the psalmist tell you about the time when it seemed God was absent. Feel the companionship of another who has yearned for God.

In the silence of today, let yourself feel that feeling of God's absence. If you need to, remember it from the past. If it is a present feeling, let it come to you.

As you remain in the silence, ask yourself some difficult questions:

Is this sense of the absence of God really a fact, or is it a feeling?

If you feel that God has left you, when did you lose the connection with him?

Is this really absence, or has God simply moved on ahead and now beckons you out of a space that has become too confining?

Have you worn out your old, familiar ways of being with God? Could God be bored with the ways you have of meeting him desire to show you something new and more appropriate for your level of maturity?

Is it possible that God is in hiding, watching to see if you want his presence or just his presents?

As you wait in the silence, your heart will give you the truth. Once you know the truth, you will know what to do next.

Even when it seems God is absent, keep affirming the reality that God is with you. God will never leave you. He will not forsake you. Breathe it and believe it.

If God wanted to show up in a new way with you, what new thing might he do?

Psalm 42:1-7

Who is responsible for your spiritual well-being, your serenity and your sobriety, either emotional or physical?

Are you looking outside yourself for the emotional and spiritual support that only God can provide? Do you wait for another human being to do for you what you should be doing for yourself?

Along the path, there are helpers, guides, teachers, counselors, and soul friends. There are people who appear at just the right time to lead you to the next phase of your spiritual formation. God uses human instruments on a regular basis to stir up faith in the hearts of his children.

God does not expect a level of maturity you have not attained, and he doesn't expect you to do for yourself what you cannot do. However, he does expect you to live the maturity you *have* attained, and he does expect you to do for yourself what you *can* do.

Often, spiritual hunger and thirst are the result of not taking responsibility for your own nurturing. Sometimes a downcast soul is the result of spiritual negligence! Soul work is hard work, and it has to be done consistently, consciously, and intentionally.

In the silence of today, be honest with yourself. Are you taking responsibility for what is yours? Are you blaming someone else for you hunger and thirst? Are you giving someone else too much power in your life?

What does God expect of you, given your level of spiritual maturity?

What do you expect of yourself? How responsible are you for your spiritual well-being?

Psalm 42:5-7

DAY FOUR

It's so easy to blame God for a downcast soul!

Today, take a look at yourself and ask if God is the problem or if he is using something else to draw you deeper into his heart.

If a human being is getting on your nerves or giving you grief, don't blame God. You can, however, use that outer stimulus to let go of your inordinate attachments and move deeper into your life with God.

If you are doing something to cause your distress, don't give God that responsibility! You can use your self-defeating habit or attitude as a lifeline to God. You can admit that without it, you might not be as interested in seeking a deeper and more intimate relationship with God.

If you have some failure or lack or limitation in your everyday life, don't blame God! Instead, surrender that emptiness or limitation to God and let him lead you into the deeper waters of life with him. Remember the disciples who fished all night, only to be asked by Jesus to put their nets on the other side of the boat, in a deeper place.

God always calls us to "launch out into the deep." He is not content that we wade around in the shallow waters near the safety of the shore. Instead, he asks us to venture into the depths of his love, the depths of his wisdom, the depths of our own strength.

In the silence, dare to differentiate between the sorrows caused by humans and the call of God who wants you to know him in all of his fullness.

Psalm 42:8

This is a verse for memorizing. In fact, keep it with you from now on, for the rest of your life. Underline it, perhaps in gold ink! Speak it to your children and to your loved ones. This is a truth that will change your life. You can count on it.

In the silence, breathe deeply and say each word slowly and carefully.

Wait in the silent space where there are no words. Be willing to experience the prison of the Living God in that silent space.

Wait and rest in the assurance of God's intent toward you, even in this present moment. As you inhale, affirm that you are drawing in the love of God, extended just for you.

When your mind wanders to a problem or duty that demands your attention, don't fight the thought. Simply return to this verse and affirm it. Stay with it for as long as you need, and notice that peace begins to fill your mind and heart.

When you want to argue with the truth of the verse and your mind offers evidence that would refute it, simply turn your mind back to the verse.

When doubt or fear interrupt the peace of the moment, return to the verse.

When your feelings counteract that feeling of love, return to the verse.

Give up any concern with whether or not the process is "working." Don't get attached to results. Don't grade your progress in prayer. Simply be in the presence of Divine Love.

Teresa of Avila said that it took twenty-nine years to learn to pray, and that most of that time, her prayers were dry and boring. How long have you been praying?

Psalm 42:9–11a

DAY SIX

God is constant. Your feelings will fluctuate. God's intent toward you remains the same. Your ability to respond to God depends on many variables.

If you feel God is absent, ask yourself some questions:

Have you had enough rest?

Is there something in your physical condition that needs attention?

Is there a problem in your relationships that you are not addressing?

Is your prayer closet really private and free from interruptions?

Are you consistent with your prayer and meditation, or do you come and go?

Is there something you don't want to face, something that keeps coming up for air, wanting to be healed?

Are you hiding something from God? Do you need to make a confession?

Is there someone with whom you need to make amends?

Are you on medication that alters your moods?

Do you need to go back and do remedial work with your concept of God and your concept of yourself?

In the silence, be willing to hear the truth. If, however, you return to a self-shaming mode, that is not where God wants you to be. If you hold shame and guilt after confessing to God, you confess to the wrong God.

If something comes between you and God, are you willing to know what it is?

Psalm 42:11b

In the practice of meditation, it is important to know your motivation. Why are you, after all, seeking union with God?

Do you want special powers? Do you hope for a dramatic light show or the bells and whistles of some ecstatic experience?

Do you seek special treatment or favors from God? Do you want to be known as a more spiritual person than the rest of the population?

Do you seek union with God out of a desire to manipulate God? Do you hope that if you seek a deeper life with God, you will somehow avoid pain and trouble, or that he will take away the pain you have now?

In the end, the only reason to draw closer to God has to be love. It is out of love and for love that we are created, and it is the love of God that draws us near.

Any benefits that grow out of that primary love relationship are gravy! Any special gifts that flow from that relationship are gifts intended to be used not for your own enjoyment, but in copartnership with God, for the redemption of the world that God loves. Any graces or consolations that come from your inner devotion to God are to be received with thanksgiving and awe, but they are not intended to give you a special run on the ladder of faith. You are blessed to be a blessing.

In the silence, ask God to show you the truth about the motivation of your heart. Always, motivation is mixed. You will not be able to know all your motives, but you can at least get clearer day by day.

If nothing were in it for you but the love of God, would you still seek his presence?

Psalm 90

Pray without ceasing.

—1 Thessalonians 5:17

Would to God that we might spend a single day really well.

—Thomas a Kempis

This is the psalm that places time in perspective. Pray this psalm and realize that your life, when compared to the vast spread of time, is but a flicker. Pray this psalm and know the urgency of each day.

Realize, too, that while you can see from the perspective of chronological time, the perspective of God is one of all-seeing and all-knowing. God's time is *kairos* time; it is the big picture.

As you take time to linger in the presence of God today, place your focus on the lifeline of your own history, as you live it out day by day. How much time do you spend with consciousness that you are in the presence of God?

What would happen to your time—the minutes and hours of each day—if you cultivated a more constant awareness of God's present help and activity, available to you at all times? *Living in the awareness of the presence of God changes everything.*

If you have not chosen a prayer word that will be your reminder and your anchor throughout the day, why not? Breathing that word throughout the day as an expression of your desire to dwell always with God somehow infuses the most ordinary tasks with a sense of the Holy. Breathing your own prayer word is a way of returning to the dwelling place of God, whether you are in the marketplace or the board room, the office suite or the laundry room.

A prayer word is not magic. It is, however, an anchor and a lifeline. What is yours?

Psalm 91:1-2

"Where are you?"

        —God, to Adam and Eve

"I'm in a good place today."

It's a catchy phrase of the pop culture, a way to talk about your inner condition or your moods. That *place* is about a state of being and not a geographical location!

The psalmist teaches us that we have a choice of where we are. We can choose to live in the presence of God, or we can choose to live as if there is no God. We also choose how we perceive God.

The psalmist knew God's "place" as the place of safety and security. Living in God's place meant, for the psalmist, living in the kind of rest that is internal. It meant living out of one's own center instead of being tossed around by what happened in the outer world. Living in God meant living in a place of strength and confidence.

On this day, take responsibility for creating your own dwelling place. Create, in your mind's eye, a picture of yourself living with God in peace and operating from that center. Rehearse your day, seeing yourself connected at the innermost level of your awareness with the Source of life.

You can, of course, choose to live in fear. You can dwell in the place of anger and resentment, looking for proof to support the position you have taken. You can dwell on worry, envy, jealousy, or greed. You can live in self-pity and you can live for external approval. Where you live really is your choice.

Ask yourself, throughout the day, the question God asked of Adam and Eve: Where are you? Stay where you want to be by praying without ceasing.

Psalm 91:3-4

DAY THREE

The eternal God is your refuge, and underneath are the everlasting arms.

—Deuteronomy 33:27

Living in the modern world has its dangers, just as living in the ancient world did. It really isn't possible to build a hedge high enough to avoid the troubles and difficulties of life. Sometimes, no matter what you do, disaster strikes, often from a direction that you least expect. Worse, there are times when trouble comes from the very place you have spent your whole life trying to avoid!

The safety of the psalms is not about the outer world. It is the safety within, the safety that rests in the assurance that no matter what happens to you in the course of a day or a lifetime, you know that God is ultimately in charge. Ultimately, there is nothing that can separate you from God.

On this day, let the assurance of God's love for you be the focus of your meditation. Rest in the assurance that whatever happens, you are never outside the loving gaze of God.

When fears and worries interrupt your connection with the presence of God, return to this Scripture. Let your chosen prayer word be the lifeline to that place of inner courage and confidence.

Remember that God is both object and Source of your courage, and not the outcome of your life. It's your choice: life in fear, or life in God.

Your job is to keep the connection with God. God's job is to keep you in his heart.

Psalm 91:5-8

"Do not let your heart be troubled. Trust in God, trust also in me. In my Father's house are many rooms; it if were not so, I would have told you. I am going there to prepare a place for you. And if I go and prepare a place for you, I will come back and take you to be with me that you also may be where I am."

—John 14:1-3

Is that Father's house with its many rooms just for the afterlife?

I don't think so!

Dwelling with God—living with God day by day—is a choice for today! It is a way of being in the world, a way of perceiving this life and a way of staying safe from the inside out.

Keep it simple as you go about your day. You really have only two choices, no matter what happens around you. You can choose love or fear. You can live in the chaos of disbelief or the harmony of true belief. You can look for evidence to support God's absence or you can look for evidence to support God's presence. It really is up to you.

As you sit in the silence, know that your trust level will fluctuate. You will relapse into the place of self-sufficiency and then, as a result, doubt and fear, but you can always come back home. Whatever far country of rebellion or fear you take yourself to, you can always return to the Father's house.

No matter how long you are gone or how wantonly you waste the Father's love, you can always come back home. And the Father is always there, waiting just for you.

Imagine God, arms outstretched, waiting to welcome you home. How does that feel?

Psalm 91:9-13

It's often at the eleventh hour that God chooses to intervene on your behalf.

It is sometimes right before you think you cannot bear your difficulty another minute that God chooses to do what you most need.

God's interventions often come in big, dramatic ways, ways so huge that you have to believe it is God! God sometimes works in ways so impressive that you stand in awe and can only declare, "Surely, the Lord is in this place!"

Most of the time, on a more regular basis, God acts in small ways, and only the person with the inner eye to see and the inner ear to hear recognizes the whispers of his grace.

Instead of focusing on what God is going to do and when he is going to do it, your task is to clear the lenses of your perception so that you can see and hear when God does act! It is God's job to act; it is your job to watch and wait. and then to see and hear and know that it is God.

For today, sit in the silence with wonderment. Choose to inquire about your own life, asking the questions that will lead you to better seeing and hearing.

What blocks your hearing and seeing?

What do you need to do to see and hear better? How can you cooperate with God's Spirit more consistently?

Buy a notebook. When you notice the synchronistic moments when God breaks through in a meaningful way, write them down! Notice, and you will see even more.

How good are you at paying attention? Is that as good as you want to be?

Psalm 91:14

It is a covenant relationship, this friendship between you and God. It is far more serious than a contract between strangers. A covenant is a dynamic agreement between parties who love and value each other.

God is eager to give you all that you need to do what he has created you to do. He is eager to help you, to come to your aid, to provide for you and protect you.

Your response is to acknowledge God, to own up to being his child, and to live as a creature with the Creator!

Imagine yourself sitting with the Creator on this day. Picture yourself in a relaxed, comfortable setting with the God who made you. Feel the intimacy of being so at home with God that you can ask him anything, tell him what you need to tell him, and then hear what he has to say to you.

As you rest with God, ask God if he knows that you love him, and then listen for his response. What about your behavior, day by day, would show God that you really do love him?

Do you love God more than you love anyone else?

Do you love God more than you love anything else?

Do you love God even when things aren't smooth between you?

Do you love God even when you don't understand his ways with you?

Do you really love God?

How well are you keeping your part of the covenant of love?

If God were to say how much you love him, what would he say? Is he right?

Psalm 91:15

DAY SEVEN

"Abide in me, and I will abide in you . . . apart from me you can do nothing . . . As the Father has loved me, so have I loved you. Now abide in my love."

—John 15

Where do you live, day by day?

What is your dwelling place, internally?

What is "home" for you?

In the silence, see yourself meeting the Living God at the doorway of your house. Watch yourself welcoming him into all the parts of your home.

Let him into the places that you haven't straightened. Let him see the cluttered closets and the rooms that need repair.

Take the Living God through the "public" rooms, the places where you meet your friends, and back into the most private places of your home. Let him in to the places you want to hide from him.

See the Living God relaxed and at home with you. Notice how comfortable he is with you in your home. Can you be that comfortable with him?

Breathe deeply in the presence of God because you are at home with him.

As you exhale, breathe out all your worries and anxieties.

As you inhale, breathe in the comfort of his presence.

As you exhale, breathe out your deepest need this day.

As you inhale, breathe in your favorite name for God.

As you go about your day's responsibilities, practice the presence of God. It is the way of inner peace and serenity. It is your rightful dwelling place. Claim it!